Assessment Education

Assessment Education

Bridging Research, Theory, and Practice to Promote Equity and Student Learning

Edited by
Beth Tarasawa, Amelia Wenk Gotwals,
and Cara Jackson

ROWMAN & LITTLEFIELD
Lanham • Boulder • New York • London

Published by Rowman & Littlefield
An imprint of The Rowman & Littlefield Publishing Group, Inc.
4501 Forbes Boulevard, Suite 200, Lanham, Maryland 20706
www.rowman.com

6 Tinworth Street, London SE11 5AL, United Kingdom

Copyright © 2020 by Beth Tarasawa, Amelia Gotwals, and Cara Jackson

All rights reserved. No part of this book may be reproduced in any form or by any electronic or mechanical means, including information storage and retrieval systems, without written permission from the publisher, except by a reviewer who may quote passages in a review.

British Library Cataloguing in Publication Information Available

Library of Congress Cataloging-in-Publication Data

ISBN 978-1-4758-5104-5 (cloth)
ISBN 978-1-4758-5105-2 (paperback)
ISBN 978-1-4758-5106-9 (electronic)

Contents

Foreword		vii
Preface		xi
Acknowledgments		xiii
Introduction		xv
1	Use Everyday Data in New Ways, by Cara Jackson, Missy Wall, Happy Miller, and Beata Thorstensen	1
2	Recognize That Context Matters, by Beth Tarasawa, Bernice Stafford, Darin Kelberlau, Susan Nolen, and Susan Cooper	23
3	Integrate Assessment and Teaching, by Cara Jackson, Scott Reed, and Kim Walters-Parker	43
4	Clarify Learning Targets, by Amelia Wenk Gotwals, Dee Fabry, and Marc LaCelle-Peterson	63
5	Use Purpose-Driven Assessment, by Kathy S. Dyer and Jennifer Hein	83
6	Joining Forces with Colleagues, by Amelia Wenk Gotwals, Denny Chandler, Melissa Spadin, and Heather Lageman	95
7	Communicate with Students and Families, by Kathy S. Dyer, Jacki Ball, Chadwick Anderson, and Alison Mund	115

Conclusion	137
References	143
Index	155
About the Editors	163
About the Contributors	167

Foreword

IN THE BEGINNING...

Let me tell you a story that will reveal why reading the manuscript for this book left me in awe. Oh my, have we come a long way over the past twenty years in our understanding of assessment as a tool for teaching and learning!

In 1979, my research team and I set out to shift the assessment spotlight from large-scale standardized testing to the classroom level of assessment. We faced very strong headwinds in this endeavor, as both the educational policy and measurement communities were holding tenaciously to a vision of excellence in assessment dominated by accountability testing. Literally no attention whatsoever was being given to the other 99 percent of the assessments that happen in a student's life, those conducted day to day in classrooms by teachers. The driving assessment model of the times was grossly out of balance, and our mission was to restore balance.

We spent the 1980s engaged in research in classrooms and schools with teachers and their students striving to understand and document both (a) the nature and role of assessment as it unfolds day to day during the learning and (b) the actual task demands and challenges teachers face in fulfilling their responsibilities in this arena of professional competence. We sought to analyze and articulate what knowledge, skills, and beliefs teachers must bring to the classroom in order to fulfill their assessment responsibilities. With those lessons in hand, then we hoped to be able to evaluate their preparedness and to find ways to help them master essential classroom assessment competencies.

Our conclusions were informative and sometimes startling. One key finding was that teachers typically spend a quarter to a third of their professional time engaged in assessment-related activities. This is a big deal for them. Further, we discovered that neither teachers nor their supervising school leaders had been trained in even the most basic principle of sound assessment practice. This left them both ill equipped and frustrated. They truly did need help.

The very good news was that we were able to complete a thorough task analysis of the demands of classroom assessment that revealed, in fact, what teachers need to know and be able to do to conduct quality classroom assessments that yielded dependable results. So we set about the task of developing appropriate professional development programs. We were developing what we called "assessment literacy."

About that time, something astonishing happened. We encountered teachers who were engaging students as the assessment partners during their learning. We immediately began to weave their ideas into our programs: sharing clear learning targets with students from the beginning of the learning, helping students understand the key elements of successful performance, teaching them the skills of self-assessment, helping them analyze changes in the quality of their work over time, and teaching them the skills of communicating to others in student-led parent-teacher conferences.

We were well into our work promoting quality assessment and student involvement when a colleague asked if I had seen the research summary by Paul Black and Dylan Wiliam from the United Kingdom revealing the very strong evidence of the positive learning effects of student self-assessment during their learning. She said they called it "assessment *for* learning." I read their research synthesis and literally shouted, "Perfect!" Imagine our glee: we were able to blend our commonsense ways of engaging students in assessment while they were learning with a rock-solid foundation of international research linking those practices to profound gains in student learning.

In 1992, we had in place all of the background we needed to create the Assessment Training Institute. Our mission was to develop and offer much-needed undergraduate- and graduate-level practical assessment training for teachers and school leaders. Again, our focus was on quality assessments and assessment *for* learning.

Along the way, we joined an international research and development community whose two-part mission was to (a) build the evidentiary basis for the power of student-involved classroom assessment as a teaching and learning tool and (b) discover practical ways to build the assessment literacy of teachers and school leaders. It turns out we became part of an international revolution in assessment thinking.

Now let me return to my opening sentence above. The sense of awe that grew in me as I read the manuscript arose from the realization that this book provides an excellent summary of the lessons we all have teamed up to learn over the past thirty years. The authors detail achievements in research and practice related to the use of assessment to *cause*, not merely measure, student learning. The chapter authors provide us with an up-to-date review of an array of relevant case studies describing how this universe of formative classroom assessment is expanding at an incredible rate.

I hope you will allow me a moment of personal reflection on the journey I have traveled. As I read this book, I found regular reference to ideas revealed in our 1980s task analysis of the demands of classroom assessment: Teachers' classroom assessment practices must arise from a clear purpose (who will use the results and how) and from clear and appropriate learning targets. Further, they must rely on quality assessments to generate dependable results that then are effectively communicated to the intended users. And I found frequent reference to and discussion of the assessment-*for*-learning idea that casts a completely new role for students in the classroom assessment process. This idea has captured our collective imaginations, has it not? I encourage you to read on into the chapters that follow to see, understand, and feel good about how much we have learned.

But we are not done. We must accept responsibility for continuing to lead a transformation of America's vision of excellence in assessment. The policy environment has changed little since 1979 in its obsessive belief we can improve schools simply with multimillion-dollar tests used once a year. We remain grossly out of balance. In addition to helping teachers become assessment literate, our challenge also includes the development of assessment literacy of those who set policy and those who make policy operational. The new insights contained in the chapters that follow reveal a promise we hold for our students. We can do better. Our mission is to deliver on that promise.

Rick Stiggins
Portland, OR
November 2019

Preface

Using assessment systems to improve student outcomes requires shared understanding and collaboration among education stakeholders at multiple levels. *Assessment Education: Bridging Research, Theory, and Practice to Promote Equity and Student Learning* presents a powerful call to action for an assessment system that advances equity and offers educators practical applications that support sound instructional decision-making.

Each chapter outlines a research-based approach that supports classroom teaching and student learning. We then draw on the expertise of various education leaders (most notably members of the National Taskforce on Assessment Education) to provide case studies of on-the-ground examples of what these strategies look like in different settings. Included are stories from the field from various perspectives—teachers, principals, district administrators, and other educational leaders. We conclude with reflection questions that provide an opportunity for readers to examine how the chapter connects to their own context.

Editors:

Beth Tarasawa, executive vice president of research, NWEA
Amelia Wenk Gotwals, associate professor, Michigan State University
Cara Jackson, associate partner, Bellwether Education Partners

Acknowledgments

The impetus for this edited volume came from a *Principal Leadership* article, "Seven successful strategies for literate assessment" (Tarasawa, Gotwals, and Jackson 2018). This piece argues that education leaders' knowledge and skills in relation to assessment, such as incorporating professional development, use of assessment data in classroom planning, and nurturing professional collaboration on matters of student achievement and instruction, are of fundamental importance for building assessment literacy among all educators. This book extends that work, equipping readers with research-driven approaches to assessment. Ultimately, shifting the focus away from the rhetoric of punitive testing back to how quality assessments can produce accurate and timely information to maximize student learning.

This book grew out of the collaborative efforts of the The National Task Force on Assessment Education, convened and supported by Northwest Evaluation Association (NWEA), a not-for profit assessment solutions organization. The taskforce was part of a multiyear effort to address critical gaps in teacher preparation to use assessment effectively.

Many of the taskforce members contributed to this book as co-authors. In addition, we benefited from the insights of Dr. Saroja Warner, senior state technical assistance director, WestEd; John David Bowman, teacher, Westwood High School and 2015 Arizona Teacher of the Year; Eddie Cuevas, academic director, Youth Policy Institute; Amy Engelhard, data steward, North Dakota Educational Technology Council; Dr. Kristin Hamilton, senior director of standards, National Board for Professional Teaching Standards;

Dr. Sarah McKenzie, executive director, Office for Education Policy, University of Arkansas; Dr. Sarah McManus, director of digital learning, Education Services for the Deaf and Blind, North Carolina Department of Public Instruction; Keith Menk, deputy director, Oregon Teacher Standards and Practices Commission; Salem, OR; Bret Miles, executive director, Northeast Colorado Board of Cooperative Educational Services (BOCES); Dr. Carlinda Purcell, assistant to the superintendent, Harrisburg School District; Dr. Meredith Ross, senior manager of student assessment and accountability, Charter Schools USA; and Dr. Kathryn Dewsbury-White, president and CEO, Michigan Assessment Consortium.

We also benefited greatly from the three key advisers who guided the work of the Task Force: Dr. Rick Stiggins, retired founder and CEO of the Assessment Training Institute; Dr. Terri Akey, director, ORS Impact; and Bernice Stafford, most recently vice president, Implementation and Education Partnerships at Evans Newton Incorporated and board chair at WestEd.

At NWEA, Kelly Goodrich, vice president of Strategic Partnerships and Business Development, championed the taskforce from its inception. We are also grateful to Christine Yankel for her support of the taskforce work, and to Holly Alexander for editing the manuscript.

Taskforce members who contributed to the book are: Chadwick Anderson, Principal, Scott Carpenter Middle School; Dr. Dee Fabry, Co-Chair, Teacher Education Department, School of Education, National University; Dr. Mark LaCelle-Peterson; Dr. Happy Miller, Executive Director of Research, Assessment, Data and Accountability, Rio Rancho School District; Missy Wall-Mitchell, Director of Accountability for School District Five, Lexington and Richland Counties; Dr. Susan Bobbitt Nolen, Professor of Learning Sciences and Human Development, University of Washington; Dr. Kim Walters-Parker, Reading Specialist, Woodford County High School; and Scott Reed, Teacher, Niles North High School.

Finally, this book would not have been possible without those educators working directly with schools, districts, and states. Thank you for your service.

Introduction

In schools and communities across the nation, assessment is playing a more significant role in the national dialogue on teaching and learning than ever before. In many of these conversations, however, assessment is seen as a dirty word. Reports indicate that our assessment systems are broken and that schools spend too much time and energy on testing students (Stiggins 2017, 3).

Critiques of assessment might stem from accountability systems that use assessments to hold schools accountable for proficiency rather than growth and penalizing schools that serve low-income students (Downey, Quinn, and Alcaraz 2019, 399). In addition, assessments may also serve as gatekeepers limiting the number of students who can receive certain educational opportunities, such as advanced coursework or gifted programs, which raises concerns about equity. In addition, parents are opting their children out of taking state-level assessments often voicing concern about the amount of time spent on testing (e.g., see Harris 2019, 23). Some of these critiques are valid, and the education community needs to work together to reconsider the role of assessment in a learning culture.

However, what is often forgotten in these conversations is that assessment can also be used in ways that can support student learning and promote equity (Stiggins 2017, 10). As the Oregon Department of Education (ODE; 2019, 13) states,

> ODE is committed to equity and sees our statewide assessments as important tools in the work of ensuring that all of Oregon's students experience excellent

educational outcomes. Our foundational assumption is that every Oregon student deserves a meaningful opportunity to learn, including students of color, students from culturally and linguistically diverse backgrounds, students who identify as lesbian, gay, bi-sexual, trans-sexual, or queer (LBGTQ), students experiencing poverty, and students with disabilities.

Similarly, the goal of this book is to highlight cases in which educational communities are successfully using assessment to promote student learning and equitable learning outcomes. The hope is that by showcasing what high-quality use of assessment can look like, educators can see how these strategies may translate into their classrooms, schools, and districts.

Before delving into these examples, however, it is important to consider why assessment is sometimes overlooked in conversations about learning and equity. There are many reasons why this omission may happen. This chapter introduces three common "myths" about assessment and a brief clarification about why these are, in fact, myths. The remaining chapters in this book will provide concrete examples that further dispel these common myths.

MYTH 1: ASSESSMENTS JUST LET YOU KNOW IF STUDENTS "GET IT" OR NOT

It is common to think of assessment as a way to determine if a student "knows" certain content. Then, once the teacher has made that determination, he or she can use that information to provide a score or grade. While this is certainly one purpose of assessment, assessments can also be a tool to support learning.

Two common categories of assessment are often conflated: formative assessment and summative assessment. Summative assessment, or assessment *of* learning, is focused on evaluating student learning after instruction has taken place. It is often summative assessment that comes to mind when thinking about assessment. However, assessment can (and should) be used for more than just summative purposes. Formative assessment is assessment *for* or *as* learning and can be defined as,

> a planned, ongoing process used by all students and teachers during learning and teaching to improve student understanding of intended disciplinary learning outcomes, supporting students becoming more self-directed learners. Effective use

of the formative assessment process requires students and teachers to integrate the following practices:

- Clarifying learning targets within a broader progression of learning;
- Eliciting and analyzing evidence of student understanding;
- Engaging in self-assessment, self-reflection, and peer assessment;
- Providing actionable feedback; and
- Using evidence and feedback to move learning forward by adjusting learning strategies or next instructional steps. (Council of Chief State School Officers [CCSSO] 2018, 1–2)

Throughout the book, chapters will illustrate how educational communities use both formative and summative assessment to support student learning and equitable outcomes.

MYTH 2: ASSESSMENTS ARE THE SAME THING AS TESTS

While "tests" are often the first thing that comes to mind when hearing the word "assessment," a balanced assessment system encompasses a wide range of methods for evaluating a child's academic, social, and emotional abilities. Broadly defined, assessment is the process of gathering evidence of student learning to inform decision-making. Gathering evidence of learning can happen through examining what students (1) say, (2) write, (3) make, or (4) do (Griffin 2007, 92).

Thus, while tests are one part of the assessment system, gathering evidence of students' abilities can take many forms, including classroom discussions, written reports, projects, and more. In fact, the most common form of assessment in classrooms is the verbal exchanges between teachers and students. These discussions may be unplanned and guided by an interesting idea or experience that a student has brought up in class. In addition, teachers often plan discussions to draw out students' thinking during activities and can use this information to inform feedback and the next steps in the learning process (Heritage 2007, 144).

Formative assessment includes the wide range of practices listed above, such as clarifying learning targets and supporting students to engage in self-assessment. Some of these practices have strong research evidence of supporting student learning. For example, students using self-assessment strategies can experience a faster rate of learning than students who do not use self-assessment strategies (e.g., see Andrade and Brookhart 2016,

13; Brown and Harris 2013, 381). Chapters provide examples of many types of assessment being used to support student learning and equitable outcomes.

MYTH 3: ASSESSMENTS ARE JUST USED BY TEACHERS

When thinking about who uses assessments, the first people who come to mind are teachers. For example, teachers use summative assessments at the end of instructional sessions (e.g., units) to determine how much their students know and are able to do. However, a fuller picture of assessment should include a larger list of people who use assessments for a wide range of purposes. For example teachers, students, parents, and administrators can use assessments to: identify what students have learned, provide insight into what students should learn next, and empower students to investigate their own learning.

As discussed earlier, teachers use formative assessment to continually monitor students' ideas and understanding throughout the day. When formative assessment is done effectively, students are also a large part of the process. Teachers can support students in better understanding the goals for learning and self-assessing to take control of their own learning. Thus, students should also be a primary user of assessment.

Educators are also becoming more proactive in communicating with families about assessment (Harvard Family Research Project 2013, 2). When teachers explain the purpose of various assessments, discuss learners' progress, and identify academic and nonacademic strengths and areas for growth, they equip family members with meaningful information to better support learning at home. Ideally, such communication about assessment evidence with families can build trusting relationships between home and school.

Given the wide range of assessments discussed earlier, many people in addition to teachers can find assessment helpful. Large state-level assessments can allow administrators to compare outcomes across schools and districts to ensure that all students receive the learning experiences that they need to be successful. Parents and teachers can use diagnostic assessment data to discuss the best ways of supporting student learning both in and out of the classroom. Principals can use assessment to determine whether curricular resources are working. Overall, assessments are designed and used to inform educational decisions at different levels. Throughout this book are examples of how various members of the educational community can make use of assessments and assessment data.

ASSESSMENT LITERACY

To combat the myths mentioned earlier, this book includes cases and examples from a range of members throughout the educational community. The collaboration between the editors and authors in this book stem from their membership in the National Task Force on Assessment Education, which was convened and supported by the not-for-profit assessment developer NWEA. For three years, this group brought together a range of stakeholders, including classroom teachers, school, district- and state-level administrators, preservice and in-service teacher educators, assessment experts, and thought leaders.

The work of the task force began with the development of a definition of assessment literacy that all education stakeholders could use to improve assessment understanding in their communities. The definition states:

> Assessment is the process of gathering information about student learning to inform education-related decisions. One becomes Assessment Literate by mastering basic principles of sound assessment practice, coming to believe strongly in their consistent, high-quality application in order to meet the diverse needs of all students, and acting assertively based on those values.

Further, the definition identifies traits of an assessment literate person:

- Understands the purpose of the assessment and how the results will be used;
- Uses the learning targets to dictate the appropriate assessments;
- Recognizes that valid results only come from quality assessments;
- Communicates clearly about assessment results to parents, students, and others;
- Creates an assessment process that motivates students and supports learning.

This definition stemmed from both research on high-quality use of assessment and, as importantly, from the task force members' experiences and encounters with the myths discussed earlier.

To support people in the education community in developing assessment literacy, members of the task force worked to develop tools, programs, and collaborations. The genesis of this book comes from one of these products—an article in *Principal Leadership* entitled "Seven Successful Strategies for Literate Assessment" (Tarasawa, Gotwals, and Jackson 2018). The three editors of this book wrote this article to share research-based, yet practical, strategies that principals could use to support their teachers in using assessment to enhance student learning.

This book is organized around the seven strategies suggested in the article. Following this introductory chapter are seven chapters based on strategies educators can use to support assessment use for student learning and equity purposes.

- Chapter 1: Use Everyday Data in New Ways
- Chapter 2: Recognize Context Matters
- Chapter 3: Integrate Assessment and Teaching
- Chapter 4: Clarify Learning Targets
- Chapter 5: Use Purpose-Driven Assessment
- Chapter 6: Joining Forces with Colleagues
- Chapter 7: Communicate with Students and Families
- Conclusion

As readers go through the case studies, the various terminologies, different vocabulary, and primary audiences may get confusing. For example, what some authors call *educators*, other call *teachers* or *candidates* depending on the case study. The ideas and messages these authors describe are far more important than the vocabulary used, and we encourage readers to look beyond minor discrepancies in terminology.

Each chapter begins with a summary of the research evidence backing the proposed strategy. Following the description of the research, one or two case studies illustrate what these strategies look like in classrooms, schools, districts, and states across the United States. These cases are provided to show how, when using these strategies, educators can combat the myths discussed earlier. We also include reflection questions at the end of each chapter to provide readers with an opportunity to examine how the chapter connects to their own setting.

While many misuses of assessment occur in the educational system today, the research and case studies in this book suggest that, when used appropriately, assessment can support student learning and equitable outcomes. We urge readers to take lessons from the chapters and see if and how they might attempt these strategies in their own contexts.

Chapter 1

Use Everyday Data in New Ways

Cara Jackson, Missy Wall, Happy Miller, and Beata Thorstensen

SECTION BY CARA JACKSON

Schools and classrooms are overflowing with information about students and their learning, and teachers continually collect and respond to evidence of student learning in a variety of ways (Tarasawa, Gotwals, and Jackson 2018). This chapter provides an overview of evidence that supports the use of everyday data as a source of information about where students are in relation to learning targets and how that data can be leveraged to help teachers and students themselves identify next steps.

Research Base for Using Everyday Data in New Ways

While test scores are one form of data, and perhaps the first type of data that comes to mind, everyday data can be gathered from the questions students ask, the dialogue between students as they collaborate, students' responses to questions, and written student work. This type of data can be invaluable in supporting students' day-to-day learning.

Holistic information about students such as extracurricular activities, interests outside of school, and attendance patterns also constitute data that educators can use to get to know their students. Students may be more likely to invest the effort needed to improve when their teacher has gotten to know them and has built trust (Wiliam and Leahy 2015, 108). The following sections describe how educators use dialogue, student work, and student self-assessment as data to improve learning and how to create contexts to support use of everyday data.

Dialogue as Data

Verbal and written responses are rich sources of information regarding where students are in relation to the learning target. Black and Wiliam (2018, 560) advocate for teachers to "steer a learning dialogue" to elicit student thinking; they view oral classroom dialogue as the core of formative assessment. Drawing on the principles of Rosenshine (2010, 12), Sherrington (2019, 28–30) identifies a number of questioning strategies intended to solicit information regarding how well students have absorbed the content taught.

Similarly, the concepts of *noticing* in mathematics and *ambitious teaching* in science focus on eliciting students' ideas and using those ideas to frame instruction (Tarasawa, Gotwals, and Jackson 2018). Researchers van Es and Sherin (2002, 573) describe three key aspects of noticing:

- identify what is important or noteworthy about a classroom situation;
- make connections between the specifics of classroom interactions and the broader principles of teaching and learning they represent;
- use what one knows about the context to reason about classroom interactions.

The term *ambitious teaching* is used to convey an approach that elicits and supports all students' thinking for the purpose of ongoing sensemaking while students participate in learning activities (Ball and Forzani 2011, 19; Lampert and Graziani 2009, 492; Stroupe and Gotwals 2018, 296; Windschitl, Thompson, and Braaten 2012, 879). Noticing and eliciting students' thinking are ways of gathering everyday data that can be used to improve instruction.

In an article that addresses the tensions between misconceptions research and constructivist views of learning, Smith, diSessa, and Roschelle (1994, 150) describe the role of eliciting students' thinking in the learning process as follows:

> We still need to have students' knowledge—much of which may be inarticulate and therefore invisible to them—accessed, articulated, and considered. . . . Instruction should help students reflect on their present commitments, find new productive contexts for existing knowledge, and refine parts of their knowledge

for specific scientific and mathematical purposes. The instructional goal is to provide a classroom context that is maximally supportive of the processes of knowledge refinement.

Eliciting student thinking is a way for teachers to gather information, enabling them to respond in ways that enhance ongoing learning (Klenowski 2009, 264).

Student Work

Student work is another piece of everyday data that can serve multiple purposes in the classroom. In the process of planning lessons, teachers can identify key moments when learning should be noticeable and plan ways to collect evidence of that learning from each student (Hiebert et al. 2007, 52). For example, short writing tasks let teachers gather responses from all students (Sherrington 2019, 33). Compared to calling on a few individual students, collecting student work from every student provides teachers with more accurate information regarding whether students learned what was taught.

Wiliam and Leahy (2015, 42) advocate for the use of samples of student work to communicate quality to the class, noting that when students notice mistakes in other students' work, they will be less likely to make those mistakes in their own work. They recommend starting with just two pieces of work, one strong and one weak. Once students gain experience comparing the quality of work, teachers can introduce more samples as the basis for constructing success criteria for student work.

Black et al. (2004, 13) advise providing opportunities for students to respond to comments as part of the overall learning process. Such opportunities are intended to communicate that assessment is *for* learning and not just *of* learning. As they state, by providing students with opportunities to respond to comments, "the assessment of students' work will be seen less as a competitive and summative judgment and more as a distinctive step in the process of learning" (Black et al. 2004, 13).

Steele and King (2006, 139) note that students' classwork and homework provide teachers with access to "a constant stream of data." As they observe, such data can be used to inform instruction. Steele and King encourage teachers to systematically gather evidence from this data, such as by identifying specific yes-or-no questions that they can use student work to answer. For example, if students are asked to show their inferences by marking up a text, teachers might look to see whether the inferences that the students made are plausible. The answers to these questions, in turn, can inform instructional steps: What topics need to be retaught? How might students be grouped to best address learning needs?

Self-Assessment to Build Ownership of Learning

Engaging students in ongoing self-assessment can help students see themselves grow and foster a sense of agency over their own success (National Task Force on Assessment Education). To self-assess their performance on a task, students must have an understanding of what "good work" looks like; in this way, self-assessment helps students internalize the success criteria. In one study, researchers found that in classrooms where teachers implemented self-assessment strategies along with other formative assessment activities, students achieved greater gains on standardized tests (Wiliam et al. 2004, 60).

Create Contexts to Support Use of Everyday Data

Teachers need support to use everyday data to inform instruction. Based on a review of research, Schildkamp (2019, 12) argues that the school leader plays a critical role in supporting data use. School leaders can encourage the use of data by framing the process as supporting continuous improvement, rather than by emphasizing accountability, and can use their own data literacy skills to monitor, model, scaffold, guide, and encourage the use of data. Schildkamp (2019, 12) recommends that school leaders distribute leadership so teachers are empowered in the data use process and believe they can take action based on data.

Additionally, instructional coaches play a critical role in providing support to teachers as they analyze student data to guide instruction. A statewide reading program in Florida middle schools paired instructional coaches with teachers. A mixed-methods evaluation of the program revealed that it is associated with both perceived improvements in teaching and higher student achievement (Marsh, McCombs, and Martorell 2010). In the case studies that follow, school leadership and instructional coaching are key supports that enable educators to use everyday data in new ways.

This chapter's two case studies highlight different types of everyday data and provide insight on how such data are used to promote student learning. In the first case study, Missy Wall describes how assessments support equity by enabling teachers to differentiate instruction to meet the needs of students enrolled in a career and technical education program. In the second case study, Happy Miller and Beata Thorstensen illustrate how one school transformed its data use process by focusing on student work and discuss how the district can support schools' use of data for continuous improvement in teaching and learning.

CASE STUDY BY MISSY WALL

This Is Not Your Father's Career and Technical Education Program

Creativity and innovation are guiding principles at The Center for Advanced Technical Studies (The Center). Teachers recognize that, just as there are multiple paths to acquiring content knowledge and skills, there are also multiple ways to measure where the student is on the learning trajectory. Everyday data in the form of personalized assessments support and guide the personalized learning. Each student is provided the specific information needed to progress.

Located outside South Carolina's state capital, The Center opened in 2012 to offer career-focused academic programs to high school students in School District Five of Lexington and Richland Counties (District 5). Students remain enrolled in their high school and take their major course of study at The Center by attending in the morning or afternoon on a double-blocked schedule. In a state-of-the-art facility, guided by highly qualified instructors with real-world experience in the fields in which they teach, students follow academic pathways not found in traditional high schools.

The Profile of the South Carolina Graduate shown in figure 1.1 shows the shared vision held by the state's education community and policy makers. The components students need to be successful after high school are organized into three areas: World Class Knowledge, World Class Skills, and Life and Career Characteristics. The instructional program at The Center is designed around this profile to ensure that all students receive the tools to be

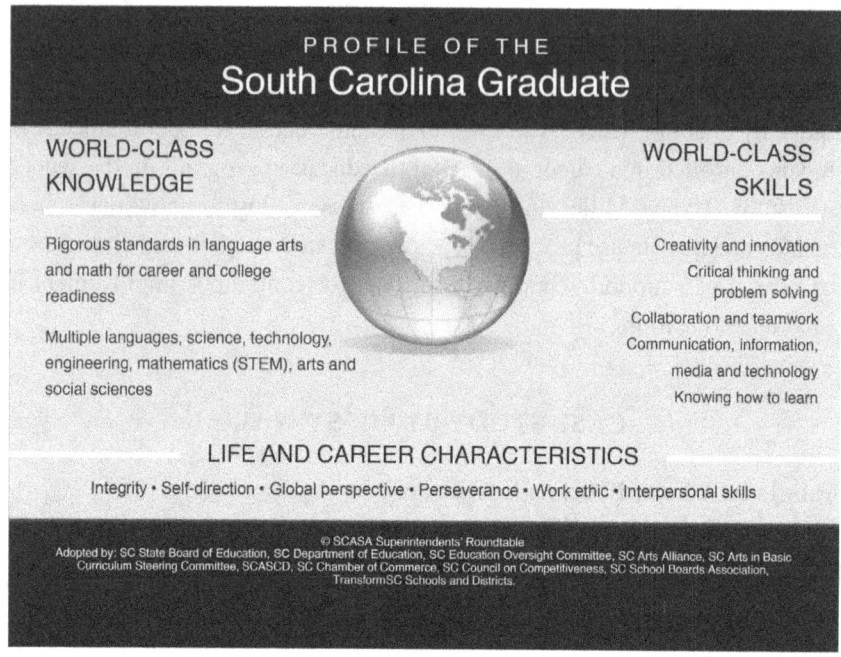

Figure 1.1 Profile of the South Carolina Graduate. South Carolina State Board of Education, South Carolina Department of Education.

successful after high school either by continuing their education or entering the world of work.

Table 1.1 lists The Center's eighteen programs of study including traditional career and technical education areas and newer technologies, such as biomedical sciences and clean energy and engineering systems. The double-blocked schedule yields the equivalent of two years of instruction compared to one academic year in a traditional schedule. Each course carries two Carnegie Units. All students are held accountable to academic and technical standards, often exceeding national expectations. In addition to academic standards, students are expected to exhibit the behavior appropriate in a professional environment.

Teachers design challenging curriculum that gives students opportunities to learn the use of technology to address problems and create solutions where no clear solution or multiple acceptable solutions exist. With an emphasis on project- and problem-based learning, students work in collaborative teams to solve real-world, often student-identified, problems with emphasis on the

Table 1.1 Programs Offered at the Center for Advanced Technical Studies

Aerospace Engineering	Electrical Design and Integrated Systems
Automotive Services	Emergency and Fire Management Services
Biomedical Science	Engineering Design and Machine Tool Technology
Biotechnology and Engineering Systems	Law Enforcement
Building Construction and Integrated Technologies	Mechatronics Systems Technology
Clean Energy and Engineering Systems	Media Technology and Visual Arts
Culinary Arts	Veterinarian Science and Technology
Cybersecurity Technology	Environmental Resource Management
Digital Art and Design	Welding Technology

application in career-related situations. Every student completes an individualized capstone project focused on developing potential solutions to a real-world problem.

Students develop written and oral communication skills by presenting their work to panels of judges and external experts. They are assessed on work ethic and interpersonal skills to assist in the development of life and career characteristics. In addition to course content and skills, students are taught how to assess their work and how to give and receive constructive feedback. Students are encouraged to take risks, learn from failures, and persevere, recognizing that the best answer often results from multiple iterations of a proposed solution.

The Center has received recognition for its innovative approach to student learning, including the National School Boards Association Magna Award and the High Schools That Work Platinum Award from the Southern Regional Education Board. Groups from across the country and international delegations have visited and seen the program in action. The shared vision at The Center is that all students will discover the intersection between their passion, purpose, and professional opportunities.

Dr. Al Gates, the current director, has served as an administrator at The Center since it opened. He began his career as a high school science teacher in 1988. As his school's department head, he implemented an award-winning science, technology, engineering, and mathematics program. In 2006 he became District 5's science curriculum coordinator. He is a certified Data

Teams trainer through the International Center for Leadership in Education and has expertise helping teachers use data to inform their instruction.

Dr. Gates compares the process of building a balanced assessment system and assessment literacy among his staff to a journey, increasing each teachers' knowledge along the assessment literacy continuum. Regardless of where they are on the continuum, the goal is for teachers and students to use a wide range of information available before, during, and after instruction.

He identifies three essential components needed to harness the potential that the effective use of data can provide. These components—a culture of trust, access to quality data, and assessment literacy—interact to create an environment in which assessment results play a role beyond an accountability tool. Teachers use formative and interim results to inform their instruction. The assessments embedded in the instructional program are to assist student learning. Educators use summative assessment results to measure the degree of learning after the instruction is completed.

Culture of Trust

The high degree of relational trust, the first component, among the adults and students at The Center fosters an atmosphere of open and honest reflection and communication. With this trust come confidence and empowerment. Teachers should be comfortable taking risks and learning from mistakes before they can ask the same from their students. Another aspect of trust is in the quality of the data and how it is used to make decisions. Inaccurate or incomplete data can lead to incorrect interpretations and can be worse than no data at all. Teachers should trust that assessment results and other information are collected and used appropriately. Everyone should understand how summative, interim, and formative assessments inform the education process.

Access to Quality Data

The second component relates to access to quality data. For teachers to take advantage of assessment results to inform their instruction, they need to have easy access to the data and time to make meaning from the information. Teachers also need technology tools to access historical student data quickly and easily from their classroom. Public schools in South Carolina have access to a Web-based student data warehouse that integrates current and historical student and assessment data. District 5 is able to provide teachers with a wealth of data, often going back to the elementary grades. From any electronic device, teachers can access their students' prior summative and interim assessment results, intervention plans, course enrollments, and grades.

For the digital tools to be of use, dedicated time must be provided for teachers to incorporate student information into their instructional planning. Wednesdays are "late start" days in District 5, when the academic day for students in grades nine through twelve begins at 10:00 a.m. Teachers dedicate their mornings to analyzing their class data in the context of recent instruction and using the information to reflect and plan. For example, after viewing the class as a whole, teachers can drill down to identify students who are struggling and to identify reasons why. Using the data warehouse, they can see interim and quarter grades the students earned in their other classes to determine if they are also struggling at their traditional school.

Instructors also use Wednesday mornings to meet together to problem solve and share instructional strategies. Teachers also use the time for individualized student conferencing focused on students' current work and progress toward their post-high school goals.

Assessment Literacy

The third component is developing capacity to use data to inform teaching and learning. The goal of continuous improvement does not apply only to the students; the school administration supports this goal for teachers as well. The unique nature of The Center and the wide backgrounds from which the teachers are drawn result in a high degree of differentiation of where each teacher falls on the assessment literacy continuum.

Teachers who transferred from one of the traditional schools in the district are typically more familiar with the summative and interim assessments than those who are new to the K–12 teaching environment. The teachers who have work-based certification serve as mentors in an apprentice environment and as such have an intuitive familiarity with informal formative assessment activities. The process of moving each teacher up the assessment literacy continuum is a focus on future professional development planning.

Teachers use a variety of direct and indirect methods of assessment. Multiple measures, both quantitative and qualitative, are used to inform teaching and learning. The Center's instructional model emphasizes collaborative project- and problem-based learning. The formative assessment practices support an iterative process of taking risks, learning from failures, and persevering, which reflects The Center's philosophy of continuous improvement.

Teachers synthesize information from computer-adaptive interim information in the data warehouse, such as Lexile reading levels, with the presented course content to refine their instructional strategies for specific students. Results of the summative assessments, such as end-of-course exams and passing rates on certification tests, are used to reflect and refine the course curriculum.

Since students are generally upperclassmen (they must be in at least the second year of high school to enroll at The Center) and have a high level of interest in the subject matter (they request the courses through their guidance counselor), they are given a greater degree of responsibility for their learning than is typically found in the traditional school setting. To the extent possible, students are expected to exhibit the behavior and attitudes expected in a work environment.

The following vignettes illustrate how multiple methods of assessments are used to inform teaching. Students take an active role in assessing their skills and use the information to improve their learning. These examples reveal an increase in rigor and responsibility on the part of the student to demonstrate and explain the mastery of content. The expectation is that at the end of the instruction, students not only demonstrate what they can do but also explain why they are doing it. The summative assessments at The Center are both written- and performance-based to reflect the practices the student will find either in college work or career certification. Where available, industry certification tests are used.

Biomedical Science: Explaining and Refining the Research Process

Students enrolled in Biomedical Science 1 and 2 experience the formal research process in a step-by-step, nonthreatening way, culminating with a presentation of their results and a paper. The project incorporates ongoing opportunities in which students gain practice thinking about their work, presenting, and explaining their reasoning. In Biomedical Science 1, students are guided through the process of developing and researching ideas of study. Each student develops two or three proposals with annotated bibliographies.

At the beginning of the second year, students create or refine their research questions. On a Wednesday morning, students may attend the CATS Café, modeled on the role coffee houses played in England during the Age of Enlightenment. During the complimentary coffee and breakfast service, students converse about their research ideas in a nonthreatening environment. Each student later presents his or her proposals to the class, and the other students and teacher provide feedback as to the feasibility of the research project, such as whether data are collectible, the student has access to necessary equipment, and the idea contributes to the field.

After students finalize their proposals, they present their research idea to a group of professionals with expertise in the field, such as physicians, university professors, and scientists from a local pharmaceutical industry. The Piranha Pond is modeled on the television show *Shark Tank*. Each student has three minutes to present their idea, and then each expert has five minutes to ask questions. Students are asked to explain how they developed their idea, why they chose it, and how they expect their project to proceed. The panel may provide suggestions or ideas to consider, and the students use that information to refine their proposal.

By midyear, each initial research plan is complete and presented in an evening poster session to students, faculty members, and advisory committee members. People ask questions one-on-one, providing students an opportunity to practice talking about their idea. Each visitor to the initial poster presentation receives a clipboard with several circle stickers and feedback forms to provide comments, suggestions, and presentation tips. The forms are collected and shared with the students at the next class meeting so that students can address the suggestions. After incorporating the feedback from the initial poster session, the students then present their information at both the district and regional science fairs, where they are judged by a group of external experts.

Most students complete a formal presentation at the South Carolina Junior Academy of Science. The poster session and a final paper written according to the style guidelines of the American Psychological Association (APA style) are submitted to the instructor, composing a portion of the final grade. Third-year students can present their completed work at the Junior Science and Humanities Symposium sponsored by the US Army. Students have also presented at the National Science Fair and the Junior Academy for the Advancement of Science.

Welding: Immediate and Specific Feedback

The initial portion of the Welding 1 course (equivalent to Welding 1 and 2 in a traditional program) starts out in the classroom environment, covering safety along with the theory, science, and concepts of welding. Students take a safety test before the commencement of work in the welding lab. No lab work is performed until the entire class has passed the test. Students who do not pass the test on the first attempt receive feedback from the instructor, in addition to targeted instruction on areas the student did not understand.

The instructor spends a considerable amount of time demonstrating the preliminary steps to welding, such as lighting the torch, adjusting the gas, and monitoring gauges. Then each student individually performs and is critiqued on these preliminary actions. The first few students are provided detailed feedback from the instructor as they go through the process. The class members use that information to refine their own understanding. As more students are able to demonstrate the steps, the instructor asks the other class members for their opinion. Students are learning to self-assess as they assess other students.

After the students have mastered the basic equipment and industry standards for safety, the instructor then demonstrates the different type of welds they will learn to do. Students then begin work in their individual booths. The small class size allows the instructor to monitor each student, observing safety guidelines and helping with technique. Once the student is confident that his or her or their work has met industry standard, the student presents it to the instructor for review. In assessing the student's work, the instructor points out areas of strength first. Aspects that do not meet industry standards are analyzed, and the instructor provides specific feedback and instruction.

The class size enables students to proceed at their own pace and receive individual or small-group instruction. When students have shown consistent mastery, they are introduced to more advanced techniques. Each student takes the state-developed, end-of-course test. Students who are successful in Welding 1 and have the instructor's recommendation may take Welding 2 the next year.

Additionally, the class size allows for high degree of differentiation and individual instruction. Students receive more complicated tasks that resemble real-world situations. Students who have mastered particular skills also participate in peer teaching. This provides them experience communicating and providing professional feedback. Peer teaching can also identify any knowledge gaps in the students who have mastered the skill.

In May, a Certified Welding Inspector is contracted to administer American Welding Society (AWS) certification tests. All students in Welding 2, and selected Welding 1 students identified by the instructor, have the opportunity to earn industry certifications. In the weeks preceding the exam, students review and practice under certification testing conditions. The instructor assesses their work using the AWS criteria and provides guidance.

The Assessment Literacy Continuum

The Center's instructional model differs from those found at the traditional high school. Some of the unique characteristics pose advantages to using data to inform instruction. The extended contact time at The Center, with a three-hour instructional period, allows teachers to immerse students in skill development. A considerable amount of instruction is through demonstration, and much of students' learning is implicit. The teachers are intrinsically able to determine the degree to which a student has mastered a particular skill.

When a student has difficulty mastering a skill implicitly, the teacher has multiple opportunities to give immediate, specific, and explicit feedback. The implicit nature of instruction encourages students to develop alternative approaches and creative solutions to problems, or to use skills in a new and different manner.

Other characteristics can pose a challenge. Teachers at The Center teach singleton courses (i.e., they are the only teacher onsite for the course), so they have fewer opportunities to collaborate with others on content-specific instructional strategies. Teachers with work-based certification are not as familiar with using traditional assessments and have less experience applying alternate sources of information to identify and address knowledge gaps. For example, if a student can demonstrate mastery of the skills for certification but is unable to pass the accompanying written knowledge test, the challenge is to use other data sources to identify the cause and develop a plan for the student to improve. All students have multiple opportunities to demonstrate mastery.

Differentiated professional development resources are offered as teachers continue along their individual assessment literacy continuum. Some activities may focus on increasing the ability to explicitly explain the implicit nature of what is taught. Others help teachers break down tasks into smaller steps to determine each of the tacit skills and knowledge required within the summative performance. Still, teachers may need resources to help with formative and interim assessment development.

This continuous improvement of assessment practice helps fulfill the collective vision that every student finds the intersection between his or her passion, purpose, and professional opportunity. The expectation of The Center is that students pass national certification tests or present a capstone project in front of a panel of experts. The instructional model supports equity by allowing teachers to use personalized learning to address each students' interests, strengths, and challenges. Teachers differentiate instruction by allowing students to work and progress independently, allowing for remediation or acceleration. While holding every student accountable for the same standard, the instructional model allows teachers to address individual needs.

CASE STUDY BY HAPPY MILLER AND BEATA THORSTENSEN

Everyday Data as a Tool to Support Equitable Teaching and Learning

Rio Rancho Public Schools (RRPS) has used state and interim assessment data and promoted a culture of data use for nearly twenty years. Use of data, such as reports from the MAP growth assessment, had become a directive and a mantra, but devoid of direction. While school leaders commonly posed questions such as "Are you examining your data at every meeting?" and "Where is your data?" to grade-level teams, the conversation usually ended there.

Teams often reexamined the same mountain of data, meeting after meeting, looking for answers to present themselves. They saw the same patterns in achievement, with no clear direction about what was most important, creating a climate of frustration and disengagement.

To tackle this challenge, educators needed a comprehensive process for walking through data, focusing less on charts and graphs and more on student work. The everyday data of student work served as a bridge that helped teachers see the connection between instructional practice and outcomes on assessments. It gave teachers regular insight into their students' progress toward proficiency and served as a form of evidence regarding whether instructional changes had the intended effect of supporting all students in reaching proficiency.

The District Process

To help teachers examine the alignment of curriculum, instruction, and assessment, RRPS implemented an online assessment management and data warehouse tool that helps staff members analyze student achievement on formative, interim, and summative assessments by standard, depth of knowledge, or item. However, simply providing access to data is not enough. Principals and teachers need comprehensive assistance in understanding the data and in using these data to inform instructional practice.

To facilitate this work, the district hired a data coach to work directly with school teams to accomplish the following:

- Help school improvement teams formulate data questions. School teams often struggle to articulate the questions they seek to answer, and therefore, struggle to figure out what data they need. This challenge may result in a dependence on data mining, in which teams look at as much information as they can, hoping that something useful will surface, rather than start with a question of interest.
- Help identify what evidence, such as student work or observations of teaching, is necessary to review the question of interest. The coach also works directly with teams to understand the operational definitions of these data, and what they *can* and *cannot* say about the critical question of interest. Assessments all measure discreet constructs, in different ways, and reporting differs across these assessments. Understanding these differences is critical to understanding student performance.
- Facilitate discussions about improvement plans. After teams analyze the data, the coach works with the teams to identify and delineate next steps via improvement plans.

The district uses processes aligned to continuous improvement best practices, specifically, Harvard University's Data Wise process. To avoid "initiative fatigue" and to ensure that processes adhere to state reporting requirements, continuous improvement facilitation protocols have been established without the official Data Wise label in RRPS. The two steps that have required the most attention in this process are the first and second steps—organizing for collaborative work and building assessment literacy.

At the beginning of the school year, teams review overall results from the summative assessment system—percentages of students in each proficiency category by subject, grade, and subgroup. The team conducts the whole group review, and very quickly. The focus of this work is to celebrate growth from one year to the next and to identify major issues to examine in detail. Next, grade-level teams review more granular data. Data are organized by grade, subdomain, and evidence statement/standard. The text of the Evidence Statement, the standard, or both appear along with the data, allowing teachers to analyze data without having to look up the language of the standards. Performance is color coded in stoplight colors to help with analysis.

Before the review, the district and school data coaches spend a few minutes centering teams in the process of evidence examination and remind them about the data limitations and threats to reliability and validity. Teams are also instructed to avoid inferential discussion statements and to ground all statements on the evidence in front of them. Teams are asked to answer two questions:

- What subdomain(s) are students struggling with the most?
- Within those subdomains, are there any discernible patterns of struggle? What are they?

The coaches give teams a simple T-chart with the headings "What do you notice?" and "What do you wonder?" and ask them to review the data as a group and take notes. Teams are given about fifteen minutes per content area to review and take notes. After teams complete their work, they report out. Commonalities across grades are identified, and as a school, instructional staff determine student-centered challenges to focus on in their initial work of the year.

While grade-level teams analyze detailed data independently, instructional staff work as a *school* to determine initial student-centered challenges. To effectively support school improvement, it is critical for schools to identify common issues. Doing so allows the district to effectively deploy resources and lets the school and district monitor progress. In short, if everyone is working on something different, it is difficult to support all educators or to tell if the changes are effective.

The district does not provide evidence by teacher for this work, and no individual teachers are called out for having done particularly well (or poorly). Whole-school change is dependent on supporting a culture of collaboration. Dividing evidence by teacher, or elevating any particular teachers as exemplars, often divides more than it unites and negatively impacts school culture.

After teams identify the student-centered challenges, they identify the measures that capture the specific skills that students need to develop. Teachers select formative assessment measures associated with the construct of interest. These measures are often assignments or other types of student work designed to provide concrete evidence of what students know and are able to do. School-level teams use this student work along with the standards to calibrate what proficiency looks like, as well as to determine what common problems students within a given grade level are experiencing.

Teachers can then collectively identify where opportunities exist in the curriculum to improve student knowledge and skills and plan differentiated groups. They plan the meetings for the semester, articulating what student work will be used as evidence and when to monitor student progress on the skills of interest.

As additional evidence of whether teachers' instruction and students' progress on skills of interest have resulted in improved performance, teachers analyze interim assessments periodically. It is this part of the process that allows data users to move beyond simply collecting and analyzing data to apply the knowledge gained and to assess the effectiveness of their instructional responses, as described in figure 1.2, Marsh's (2012, 2) data use theory of action.

Sandia Vista: A Model of the Process at the School Level

Sandia Vista Elementary School, an elementary school with approximately 700 students within RRPS, started using data in new ways three years ago and has become one of the highest-performing elementary schools in the district. Under the guidance of the school's administration and instructional coach, the staff start the beginning of the year by analyzing the results of the state accountability exam and spring interim assessment data to find the

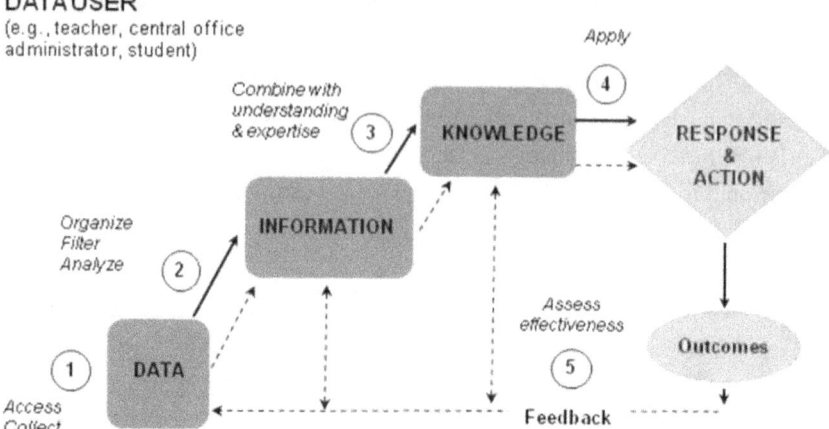

Figure 1.2 Data Use Theory of Action. Marsh, Julie A. 2012. "Interventions Promoting Educators' Use of Data: Research Insights and Gaps." *Teachers College Record* 114 (11): 2.

overarching indicators of instructional needs. They look for trends across grade level and within the domains of the standards. This data is used to build and align the school continuous improvement plan, grade-level goals, and teachers' individual professional development plans.

By the beginning of October, the teaching teams examine data from the fall interim assessments to determine both grade-level trends and individual classroom needs. This type of data analysis is typical within many schools across the nation. However, the teachers at this school then use this data to identify four to five students from every classroom who are in the *projected proficient* range on the interim assessments who also consistently perform well across a variety of classroom measures. The work produced by these students becomes the focal point for school-wide instructional planning, the North Star of what proficiency should look like for *all* students.

According to Elise Gibbs, the school's instructional coach, the teachers look at how the students within this focus group fall within the learning continuum from the interim assessments and how the skills listed on the learning continuum, as areas of need for further instruction, relate to the curricular scope and sequence within the Tier 1 curriculum teachers are providing for all students. She states:

> We have spent the past three years trying to define proficiency. I have found that many teachers perceive these students as high, when in fact they are performing

at grade level expectations based on the assessment and curriculum. Using the learning continuum alongside the curriculum has really helped clarify that these students are where we want everyone to be. It has also helped us leverage the curriculum as a partner for reaching our students' needs.

In November and December, the teachers bring sample work from everyday instructional assignments and assessments for their focus students to their weekly collaborative meetings. The sample work includes common curriculum-embedded, performance-based assessments and mid-module assessments as well as exit tickets and some samples of daily instructional assignments.

During the meetings teachers identify trends and gaps in the students' understanding both within and across the classrooms at their grade level. Examples include identifying specific skill gaps in knowledge like creating number line plots within the focus area of multistep math processes and using appropriate descriptive language within narratives.

Within their schoolwide instruction planning, teachers make sure that they include explicit instruction not only to meet the needs of these students but also to provide grade-level instruction for all students within the class. Then the teachers examine the work samples of a second group of students who are not yet *projected proficient* to identify the differences in instructional needs. As Patricia DiVasto, the school's principal, states, "Everyday data is more than just numbers and scores. It gives us strong insight into understanding how best to support our students."

Teams use the identified focus groups as their exemplar for schoolwide, high-quality instruction throughout the year. In January, the teaching teams examine the new interim assessment data, focusing especially on growth within the grade level and each classroom. Teachers are encouraged to visit each other's classes to observe teaching methods. During the spring semester, the teaching teams work with the instructional coach, special education instructional leader, English language coordinator, and student assistance team chairs to examine how students with different needs are accessing the schoolwide instruction and also to plan for targeted and individualized instruction.

These observations and discussions of typical "everyday" formative assessment and differentiation of instruction processes provide invaluable insight for teachers as to how they can better meet the needs of the students within their own classroom. At the end of the year, the teams use the data to monitor their progress on the school's improvement plan and to begin planning for instruction and professional learning for the following year.

Gibbs states that the teacher response to using interim and summative data to identify focus areas and then using related everyday student work for instructional planning has been very positive: "Data is not as scary anymore. It has context and it feels actionable. We know how to respond to student work but we don't necessarily know how to respond to a number on a chart. This work builds a bridge between numbers and instruction."

Lessons Learned

The district learned several lessons from engaging in this process. First, traditional assessment data can provide *look-fors*, but student work provides greater insight. For example, assessment data might show that students are struggling in writing, and evidence statement analysis can even highlight challenges in specific areas, such as compare and contrast.

Yet to truly understand what instruction students need, teachers must get elbow-deep in examining student work. That is where teachers learn whether students are struggling to understand the prompts, comprehend the text passages that they are responding to, or organize their thinking in logical ways. These specific issues are infinitely easier to address than attempting to tackle writing in general, as they provide the direction for future instruction.

Second, less can be more. One of the biggest *aha* moments in using data to improve instruction was that educators had to stop hunting for the biggest levers for improvement. In essence, educators had to give themselves permission to say, "We have any number of instructional areas to improve. Pick *one*." The key to building momentum in using assessment data to improve instruction is to build agency in teachers to select the instructional area they wish to tackle as a school. The key is to *start*.

Similarly, good continuous improvement work does not require the analysis of mountains of data to get underway. Traditional wisdom about "data triangulation" can readily lead into data overload, and accountability pressures have led to a healthy distrust and dislike of the data analysis process. RRPS's district assessment team view their job as to support teachers' data use by ensuring data are valid and accurately reflect the constructs of interest to create an efficient process of identifying areas for instructional improvement.

Third, building a culture of trust and minimizing the burden on teachers can support effective use of data to improve instruction. It is not simply about carving out space and time for teachers and principals to work together to examine data; teachers have to trust each other and their administrators to undertake the hard work of amending instruction.

Additionally, teacher teams can waste tremendous amounts of time organizing and color coding interim and summative assessment data by hand, which may not contribute to their overall understanding of what students know and are able to do. RRPS believes that organizing and summarizing data should be the work of the district and does everything it can to create consumable data reports for teachers. This allows teachers to spend the majority of their time on student work and collectively planning instruction.

Finally, one of the biggest, and continuing, challenges the district has faced is assessment literacy training. Assessments often evolve, and over time, the district has found that traditional, sit-and-get professional development in assessment literacy fails to meet the needs of end users. Without immediate use, the information is readily forgotten.

Instead, relying on the principles of adult learning theory, assessment literacy is delivered in situ, as school teams are examining their own data. This informs immediate decision-making and makes assessment literacy more relevant to daily use. When any data session is launched, facilitators spend a few minutes reviewing the assessment constructs. They discuss what the assessment *can* and *cannot* measure, given when the assessment is administered, limitations due to sample size, and other issues. This just-in-time review provides users with the information they need to interpret the results in front of them.

REFLECTION QUESTIONS

1. What types of everyday data do you have in your district or school that you can incorporate into your continuous improvement processes?
2. How can you build or articulate the coherence across multiple types of data in your district or school?
3. Three components needed to harness the potential of the effective use of data are a culture of trust, access to quality data, and assessment literacy. What can you do to ensure these components are in place?
4. How are you supporting the continuous improvement of assessment practices though the use of differentiated profession development?

Chapter 2

Recognize That Context Matters

Beth Tarasawa, Bernice Stafford, Darin Kelberlau, Susan Nolen, and Susan Cooper

SECTION BY BETH TARASAWA

School systems across the country have rolled out comprehensive assessment initiatives, accountability policies, and data dashboards all in an effort to improve student performance. Teachers' use of assessment data to inform instruction is increasingly becoming common educational practice.

Yet many studies show inconsistent assessment data use among teachers, as well as a lack of preparation and skills required to interpret and use student data (Sun, Przybylski, and Johnson 2016, 28). As Stiggins (2017, 21–22) argues, "If we are to fulfill an expanded mission that now includes universal academic success in certain achievement arenas, then our assessments must deliver far more than evidence for grading, sorting, and weeding out. They must also become teaching tools—tools that motivate all students and promote maximum success for all."

However, we must recognize the political and organizational contexts of schools that shape processes of assessment data use. More specifically, research suggests that the provision of structured time, access to data systems, instructional leadership exerted by district and school leaders, and a culture of professional community are important organizational context conditions for teachers' collaborative assessment data use (Farley-Ripple and Buttram 2014, 50). Coburn and Turner (2011, 176) provide a useful framework (shown in figure 2.1) for organizing research on data use and underscore the importance of understanding the conditions that promote assessment use in schools.

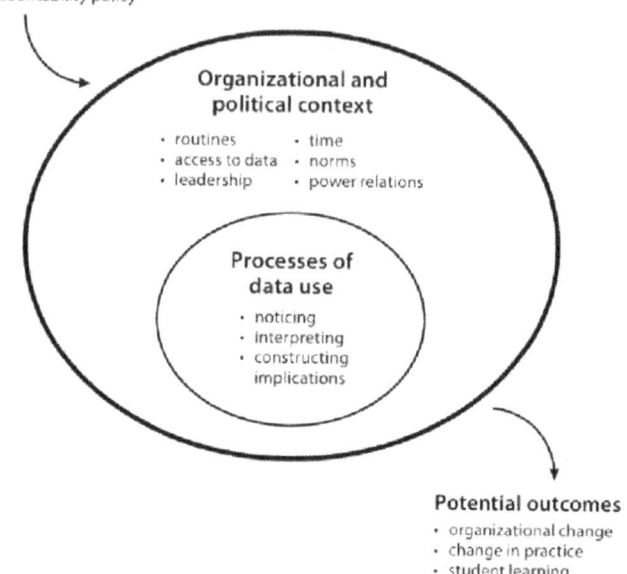

Figure 2.1 Coburn and Turner's Framework for Data Use. Coburn, Cynthia E., and Erica O. Turner. 2011. "Research on Data Use: A Framework and Analysis." *Measurement: Interdisciplinary Research & Perspective* 9 (4): 176.

Coburn and Turner (2011, 180–85) highlight four primary organizational and political context factors that shape assessment data use. These factors include how the scheduling of time, availability to data, organizational norms that guide interactions, and the influence of power and authority influence routines.

First, assessment data use routines, or ways that people interact with data and one another, shape how the process of data use progresses by focusing and framing educators' attention as well as influencing one another in social interaction. These routines may be formal and highly structured, such as professional learning communities with guided protocols or facilitated by a coach or principal, while others may be less formal. The defining feature for a data use routine is that it is a reoccurring and patterned collaboration that influences how people engage with one another and the assessment data (Coburn and Turner 2011, 181). Routines are further affected by the amount of time devoted to assessment education and data use.

Second, the technological infrastructure (e.g., data collection, storage, and retrieval) and human infrastructure (i.e., how individuals through the organization are connected to each other) impacts the accessibility of data (Coburn 2010, 181–82; Honig 2003, 332–33; US Department of Education 2010, 9–28).

School norms also guide interaction with assessment information. Schools that establish norms that empower teachers to openly share data about their classroom practice, critique each other, and encourage peer-to-peer shadowing are more likely to foster conversations that tackle issues of instruction and student learning (Timperley 2009, 78–79). District and school leaders play a vital role in the choices they make to select or design assessment data use routines, how they configure time, who gets access to what data by establishing norms of interaction, and how they participate in assessment use themselves (Coburn and Turner 2011, 183). Finally, differences in authority and power can influence the interpretive process and instructional decision-making among teachers and building or district leadership (Coburn, Bae, and Turner 2008, 377).

The RAND Corporation's American Educator Panels survey (Tsai and Tosh 2019) provides additional insight into teachers' self-reported contexts, their access to assessment data, and the supports they receive in using student information to guide decisions about instruction. The majority of teachers report having received support with using data. The three most common supports are principal encouragement for using data in decision-making (64 percent), professional development offered at their school site (59 percent), and support from a consultant or a school or district staff colleague skilled in data analysis (45 percent) (Tsai and Tosh 2019, 2). Less frequently mentioned supports include professional development offered outside of school, formal coursework covering assessment use in decision-making, and paid time for examining student data to guide decisions about instruction.

Another influential body of research identifies common interpersonal conditions found to affect successful assessment data use interventions. Most notably, Marsh's (2012, 12–17) review of the literature finds that a school's climate of collegiality and trust can be a prerequisite for facilitating data use. Groups with trusting relationships experience more progress in using assessment data and attaining desired results than those without trusting relationships (Nelson and Slavit 2007, 37).

Moreover, the US Department of Education (2010, 71) reports that when teachers look at data collaboratively, the importance of mutual respect and a culture of continuous improvement is a persistent condition to facilitate data use. But Marsh (2012, 16–17) also cautions leaders and educators to be mindful of potential difficulties (e.g., competing needs, providing necessary technical support, and limited resources and capacity) when trying to support a culture of data use.

This chapter highlights two case studies that discuss how the organizational and political contexts in districts and schools shape assessment data use processes. We first turn to Nebraska where Millard Public Schools demonstrates how establishing structured time and providing professional learning opportunities are defining features of its student-centered assessment system. Here, Bernice Stafford and Dr. Darin Kelberlau chronicle how assessments can support accountability and program evaluation, while enabling teachers to have access to actionable information they can use with students.

We then hear first-hand accounts from novice and veteran teachers on how they negotiate assessment practice with students, colleagues, and administrators. Dr. Susan Nolen and Dr. Susan Cooper explain how teachers must deal with audiences both inside and outside the school district when engaging in assessment practice.

CASE STUDY BY BERNICE STAFFORD AND DR. DARIN KELBERLAU

Millard Public Schools

State and district assessment systems are not intended to function in isolation. Instead, the expectation is for assessment systems to support multiple purposes of which curriculum and instruction are high priorities. However, unless assessments are implemented effectively in schools and classrooms, and teachers are trained in their use, the intended purpose of support for teaching and learning will not be realized. The effectiveness of an assessment or assessment system "in improving learning depends on its relationships to curriculum and instruction. Ideally, instruction is faithful and effective in relationship to curriculum, and assessment reflects curriculum in such a way that it reinforces the best practices in instruction" (Pellegrino, Chudowsky, and Glaser 2001, 221–22).

Assessment is context sensitive—classroom use by students and teachers and program evaluation and accountability by administrators and policy makers. For assessment to be effective in any context, users must be assessment literate (Pellegrino, Chudowsky, and Glaser 2001, 225–30).

In 2016, the Nebraska Department of Education (NDE) unveiled Nebraska Quality Education Systems for Today and Tomorrow (NEQuESTT) that aligns with Accountability for a Quality Education System Today and Tomorrow (AQuESTT). This document articulates a comprehensive vision and direction of an educational system ready to provide support to every student as needed.

In June 2019 NEQuESTT was strengthened with the addition of stakeholder engagement and equity. Nebraska State Board of Education (2018) explains, "With an intentional and comprehensive focus on ensuring a reduction in educational inequities for the most vulnerable populations, NEQuESTT directs focus on student- or client-centered outcomes, high-quality opportunities, and a strong system of support for every student, every day." Key strategies include "using assessments to measure and improve student achievement and inform instruction . . . and goals and benchmarks that measure disaggregated data to ensure equity and access."

To support this direction, the NDE implemented its comprehensive assessment system, Nebraska Student-Centered Assessment System (NSCAS). This holistic view of assessments supports state and district accountability and program evaluation and gives actionable information they can use during instruction to provide students with timely feedback.

The design of NSCAS integrates Marion's (2018, 45) view of a comprehensive assessment system coupled with the state's Multi-Tiered Systems of Support (MTSS) framework. It connects accountability, intervention, standards-based teaching and learning, general education, and special education system-wide. When implemented in districts and schools as designed, the system serves "all important users and purposes well, informing key decision makers in formative, assessment FOR learning, and summative decision contexts using continuous classroom, periodic interim benchmark, and annual assessments" (Stiggins 2018, 5–7).

Millard Public Schools' comprehensive assessment system is an example of NSCAS implementation in suburban Omaha, Nebraska. The district enrolls more than 24,000 students in prekindergarten through twelfth grades. Twenty-one percent qualify for free or reduced-priced lunch, 12 percent have a verified disability, and 1.6 percent are English language learners.

Millard is a high-achieving school district offering many programs of choice including a Core Knowledge Program—an accredited Montessori program through eighth grade—the only Primary Years Programme (PYP), Middle Years Programme (MYP), and Diploma Programme (DP) International Baccalaureate program in the state; Early College High School; Career Academies; Air Force Junior ROTC; and an alternative school for nontraditional learners. The district also offers a one-to-one device program for all students in third through twelfth grades.

Included in the design of Nebraska's and Millard's comprehensive assessment system are classroom-level formative assessments. The state and district acknowledge these instructional support assessments are primarily a school- and classroom-level responsibility with classroom teachers responsible for their design and use. Millard administers a number of assessments between kindergarten and twelfth grade to ensure students master the knowledge and skills necessary for personal excellence.

"Formative assessments check for student understanding during instruction. Given as needed, daily in the classroom throughout the year to help teachers address student learning needs in-the-moment" (Nebraska Department of Education, Fall 2018). To support the use of classroom-level assessments, the NDE provides an online test-creation tool that classroom teachers can use to create their own formative assessments.

The NDE, at no charge, also provides an interim computer-adaptive growth assessment (NWEA's MAP® Growth™) to districts and schools for use with their choice of other interim assessments. These assessments are administered throughout the year to allow students, parents, and educators to track growth toward proficiency levels, identify learning needs, and predict performance on the state summative assessment. Millard designed and implemented Nebraska NSCAS to satisfy the district need for accountability, program evaluation, and teaching and learning.

Millard also recognizes and supports educator professional learning as integral to successfully educating students. With this in mind, the district provides across-the-board professional development programs for novice and experienced teachers alike. The district's teacher assessment literacy training incorporates the linkage of adult learning principles to the problems of practice, enabling teachers to visualize and integrate new strategies learned as they gauge their effect on student success in classrooms.

Take, for example, training in the development and use of rubrics, which are used to formatively measure student progress in writing and secondary mathematics. The district's professional learning emphasizes the importance of consistent descriptions of performance and explicitly stated attributes when using rubrics. "Professional competence and the application of new professional learning is enhanced when the learning takes place in context and improves one's micro and specific teaching skills rather than one's generic teaching skills" (Cole 2004, 7–9).

Millard's assessment literacy training is provided by two departments: the Curriculum department and the Assessment, Research and Evaluation department. The latter is the lead in providing technical support to the Curriculum department Teacher Leaders who are the face of training in the district. Teacher Leaders are guided through an extensive process that includes development of district curriculum frameworks aligned to state standards, course guides, pacing maps, and the relationship of these resources to district assessments.

In turn, Teacher Leaders replicate their training and extend it throughout the district as they work with classroom teachers. Because of the nature of this work, the training that classroom teachers receive is an involved process that supports the overall success of assessment literacy in the district.

The primary vehicle for professional development in the district is the professional learning community (PLC)—a structure that encourages staff innovation and personalized learning through peer collaboration within the school and classroom environment. School-level PLC structures are sensitive to context, enabling individual learners "to be exposed to a range of opinions and approaches grounded in a shared experience of the school" (Cole 2004, 7).

The district characterizes its PLC teams as groups of results- and data-focused district and school professionals whose mission, vision, values, and goals are shared as they meet regularly in collaborative teams where the focus is on action-oriented learning and continuous improvement (Millard Public Schools 2018). A typical assessment literacy school-level PLC meeting will find classroom teachers jointly analyzing the work of students and identifying their learning challenges as they set goals align with the content standards being taught (Mishkind 2014, 1–3).

Millard is similar to most school districts implementing a coherent and comprehensive assessment system in that its effort is a work in progress with educator professional learning ongoing. With component parts (formative, diagnostic, interim, summative) in place, the focus shifts from design to continuous and ongoing development of teacher understanding and use of appropriate assessments in their instruction. District and school administrators are committed to the phased implementation of assessment literacy professional learning in these primary areas. More specifically, professional learning includes such topics as essential learner outcomes, opportunity to learn, bias, appropriateness, validity, reliability, and standard setting.

Essential Learner Outcomes reflect what students in Nebraska should know and be able to do across their entire educational experience to meet the challenges they will face in the next phase of schooling or career. The Teacher Leader members of the design team were required to identify and recommend outcomes that the district would assess based on state and local standards resulting in an assessment robust enough to cover the desired elements of each skill.

To accomplish this task, the team established a two-phase approach: initial focus on the integration of curriculum, instruction, and assessment and identifying learner outcomes, followed by deciding which standards need to be assessed at the district level. Key factors considered included identifying skills on the state assessment, critical at the next grade level, vital in multiple content areas, and associated with grade-level (or course) success. Following this step, the team determined the most appropriate way to assess the standard and review the concept sufficiently. Finally, the standard was unpacked, denoting the verb within the standard to ensure the assessment is at the intended level of rigor.

The concept of *Opportunity to Learn* is covered. Consistent with the equity strategy outlined in NEQuESTT, in their delivery of training Teacher Leaders work to ensure classroom teachers have the knowledge and training in assessment to enable each of their students to receive equitable opportunities to learn. The questions that the design and delivery team asked included the following:

- Are there sufficient opportunities for teachers to collaborate and learn together?
- Is the amount of time students are spending with the content or subject matter appropriate for the content, subject matter, or grade level?

- Is the district/school ensuring each student a high-quality learning experience by providing teachers with up-to-date curriculum frameworks, course guides, and pacing maps?

This aspect of the process aided in determining the appropriate timing for the assessment. Instruction for students with special considerations such as those receiving special education services or English language learners is also reviewed for appropriateness.

District assessment literacy training includes *Bias*. There are myriad opportunities for bias to appear in teacher-developed assessments such as when writing prompts and scoring student writing. Most bias tends to be cultural, but item and language bias may also exist. To mitigate bias, Teacher Leaders guide classroom teachers in how to write quality assessment items and recognize bias from the perspectives of fairness and sensitivity. The training also includes rich discussions about what it means when students miss an item. Is the reason they lack the knowledge and skills being measured, or should other factors be considered?

With respect to *Appropriateness*, training emphasizes these areas: (1) whether the items are written at the appropriate level for the standard and (2) whether the items or tasks are appropriate at this grade level. Also included is the use of resources such as readability formulas when the assessment involves a sizable amount of text for students to read. The training conversation factors in the when and why of rubrics over a multiple-choice editing test as the more appropriate tool when assessing collaboration, innovation, and engagement (Herman, Osmundson, and Silver 2010, 52–54).

Validity is specific to the situation. Even if a test is reliable, it may not be valid. For example, consider the quality of information a teacher receives from a multiple-choice editing test versus a rubric when measuring student progress in writing. Which assessment provides teachers and students with the more accurate and actionable information? To be valid, a well-designed item or assessment is consistent and produces comparable outcomes over time and between different students and teachers.

Reliability focuses on the need for consistency of scoring across school buildings and classrooms. Most notably Teacher Leaders cover reliability during rubric training that involves assessing student writing and the secondary mathematics course. A set of consistent district expectations in writing and mathematics is shared with teacher Raters to guide their work. Writing assessment training requires that Raters successfully complete "gateway" papers before they are eligible to score student work. To honor partial credit in mathematics, Teacher Leaders introduced a four-point score rubric for all mathematics items with scoring guidelines for each score point to ensure high levels of consistency across classrooms.

The district lead for the *Standard Setting* process is the Assessment, Research and Evaluation department supported by the Curriculum department. This hand-in-gloves departmental relationship establishes the context for all assessment-related training and the setting of district-level expectations. Because the leadership of these two departments values their important collaboration, each contributes appropriate content from their respective areas of expertise to aid classroom teachers in building assessment knowledge and skills that maximize student academic growth.

Next steps involve both departments collaboratively reviewing progress to date and acknowledging areas where more work is needed. Because of limited resources, including teachers' lack of time and insufficient training resources during the school day for face-to-face professional learning, the district plans to implement an online, virtual learning solution in the 2019–20 school year.

By taking advantage of existing district and school PLC structures, the prevalence of electronic devices, and emerging applications for efficiently collecting and scoring student writing and secondary mathematics assessments, the district will implement an internal website to house assessment literacy training modules developed by Teacher Leaders. Soon this high-touch, high-tech, on-demand, 24-7 repository of assessment literacy resources will be available to Teacher Leaders, classroom teachers, and administrators in the district on an as-needed basis for independent study or during PLC collaboration.

> Millard Public Schools is an example of what can happen when people come together for a single purpose—in our case, a world-class education for each student. It is this base of knowledge and skills that are vital to our students, and not just for what it will allow them to do, but what it will let them believe. Education is hope. It is the link between dreams and reality. It is important for our students to be able to find the correct answers. It is much more important for them to have the confidence that they will be able to continue to find those answers long

after they graduate. The education we give our students today becomes the hope that sustains them for many tomorrows to come (Millard Public Schools 2018).

CASE STUDY BY SUSAN NOLEN AND SUSAN COOPER

Contexts of Assessment Practice: Teachers Negotiating Assessment Practice

Teachers do not make decisions about their assessment practices in a vacuum. On the contrary, when establishing and modifying their practices, they must negotiate with colleagues, administrators, parents, students, and others who make use of the products of those assessments (Moss 2003, 14–16; 2008, 239; Spillane and Miele 2007, 57–61).

Assessment products (e.g., grades, test scores, portfolios) function as *boundary objects* in educational systems (Nolen 2011, 319; Nolen et al. 2011, 88). They communicate important information across the boundaries between constituencies or communities of practice (Bowker and Star 1999, 15–16; Star and Griesemer 1989, 392–93). A course grade that is created in one context (the classroom), for example, communicates some form of competency to people and groups outside that classroom: students, their parents, their future teachers, college admissions boards, and the like. Each group interprets that information in its own way, which may not reflect the ways in which that grade was produced or the values of those who produced it.

Because assessment results are used by others sometimes far removed from the classrooms in which they were created, teachers take into account those needs when choosing and implementing assessment practices, making decisions based on assessment data, and communicating with external audiences. In educational systems and their external constituencies, assessment products have implications for selection and promotion, as indicators of teacher expertise, and as evidence of school or district "success." Power relations and interdependencies within these systems mean that teachers need to negotiate their assessment practice with others. The authors draw on data from two studies, a longitudinal study of novice teachers (Nolen 2011, 319; Nolen et al. 2011, 88), and a study of teachers' grading practices (Cooper 2017, 26–41), to illustrate the extent to which assessment practice is embedded in contexts.

Novice Teachers

In an ethnographic study of novice teachers, researchers (Nolen et al. 2011, 88) observed and heard about negotiations with a variety of constituencies as three social studies and four math teachers transitioned from their student teaching placements and university classrooms to their first (and sometimes second) paid teaching positions.

Each time the teachers entered a new school community, they had to negotiate their assessment practices and the local meanings of assessment products (such as grades and test scores) with those other interested parties—the recipients and users of grades, test scores, and other assessment products. They also had to negotiate differences between their current approaches with whatever shared assessment practices the other teachers in those schools had already negotiated. If giving weekly individual quizzes, midterms, and final exams were common across most courses in a department, for example, teachers were likely to take up at least a version of that practice.

Teachers have other ways of assessing (group projects, portfolios, or performances), valued in their university teacher education program, that might be seen as disruptive to departmental norms or as producing less valuable products. All of the teachers in the study reported negotiating both overall approach and specific assessment practices with others, although there was variation in how negotiable those practices were.

Internal Negotiations about Assessment Practices and Products

Novice and newcomer teachers negotiated their assessment practice "in-house" with their students, colleagues, and administrators. Although these negotiations were likely more frequent and visible because teachers were new to their communities of practice, they likely reflect the kinds of negotiations that all teachers have as expectations, structures, personnel, and relationships shift over time.

Students

Teachers negotiated their assessment practice, for formative and summative, with the students in their classrooms. Abe,[1] a math teacher, found that students initially resisted his attempts to probe for deeper understanding through questioning during class. In one observation, a student protested his insistence on explanation by exclaiming, "I don't think about why it works! I just think about how to get to [the answer]!" (Nolen et al. 2011, 107). In this case, Abe explained his reasons for probing and continued to push.

Hilary, a social studies teacher, reported that students sometimes critiqued her directions for a task. She said, "They know what good directions look like; they expect a rubric with everything. So, if I forget something or don't do something or aren't clear enough with my directions, they will call me out on it" (Nolen et al. 2011, 107). Hilary saw this as enforcing shared school norms and adjusted her practice accordingly.

Teachers

Negotiation with departmental norms sometimes provided resources for broadening and deepening teachers' assessment literacy. Gemma, a social studies teacher, had resisted the development of scoring rubrics in her university assessment class, claiming that real teachers would never spend that amount of time and effort.

When she became a certified teacher, she found that the development, use, and revision of scoring rubrics was an important assessment practice in her new department. Becoming a member of that department, in her view, required shifting her position on rubrics. The conversations and resource-sharing with teacher colleagues provided opportunities and resources to refine her skills and learn the value of well-constructed rubrics in producing useful information for teachers, students, and parents.

Novices sometimes resisted existing practices and feared their influence on their own assessment approaches. Although Brett, a second-year high school math teacher, met frequently to discuss teaching with his departmental colleagues, he resisted their valued practice of developing common assessments. "One of the things that they're really focused on right now is common assessments. And I've kind of shied away from that whenever they want to meet on that; I try to be busy that day" (Nolen et al. 2011, 114). His resistance stemmed from the other teachers' use of "traditional tests," which he found inappropriate and did not want to adopt.

Administrators

Because of their power to influence decision-making, administrators often played a role in negotiations with novice or newcomer teachers. While he was a student, one novice social studies teacher, Karl, had dismissed the importance of emphasizing writing skills. He told his classmates that scoring writing in social studies placed "unnecessary emphasis on conventions" and that he wanted a student with "mediocre grammar" to "still get a 4.0" (Nolen et al. 2011, 115).

As a practicing teacher, he was observed and evaluated by his assistant principal, who asserted that Karl needed to develop a standard rubric for writing assignments in his social studies class. "Once you have a writing rubric, you don't have to change it each time," the assistant principal told him and offered to give Karl the rubrics he had used for writing in social studies. In this evaluative setting, Karl agreed that such a rubric "should be part of every lesson." Later, trying out the practice, he became more convinced of its value to him as a teacher and worked to incorporate it into his practice.

Negotiations with External Audiences for Assessment Products

Teachers must also deal with external audiences when engaging in assessment practice. Some teachers reported considering parents' reactions when grading and expressed reluctance to endanger their positions as new teachers by incurring the wrath of parents. The collective impact of individual grades on students and their parents also concerned administrators.

Hilary practiced in a school established to prepare students from traditionally underrepresented groups for college success. When she had a high initial failure rate in her classes, the principal called her to account. She reported her principal as saying, "You can't have half your students failing in your class. Because if they fail, at the end of the year or trimester [unclear] they have to have a 70% or above average for all of their classes to graduate to the next class. And that's pretty big. It just doesn't look good. And I agree, it doesn't, to have half the students failing" (Nolen et al. 2011, 109).

Negotiation is a two-way street, and individual teachers can also influence the systems in which they teach. In his second school, Karl was positioned as someone with assessment expertise by his principal. She observed, "Karl brings a voice to the table that's really useful to somebody like me. Because I'm trying to have a paradigm shift in the [school] community. I really want these people to start thinking about educational practice in a way that makes good sense for student learning" (Nolen et al. 2011, 116).

In part because of their assessment preparation in their teacher education program, the novice teachers in the study were able to critically evaluate and take up local practices and also to contribute to the developing assessment literacy of their colleagues.

Grading Practices: Negotiating Multiple Local and Distal Assessment Contexts

In US education, grades are considered a time-honored and necessary tool for supporting the goals of learning and preparing students for life in the "real world" after formal schooling ends. Grades serve as communication to families and other community members (i.e., school and district personnel, policy makers, and others) about the quality of education children are receiving. Grades are often gatekeepers—determining courses of study, scholarships, and opportunities for higher education. In Advanced Placement (AP) courses, grades are presumed to represent an assessment of students' achievement at the college level.

Despite the importance of grading, few studies have looked at grading practices in situ, relying instead on teacher self-reports. In her study of AP teachers' grading practices, Cooper (2017, 26–41) interviewed and observed five teachers as they produced semester summary grades for students in their open-access AP Environmental Science course. Teachers "thought aloud" to provide insights into their thinking that show how they negotiated multiple contexts of assessment. The study is unique in that all five teachers used the same curriculum and the same assessments within the same district grading system, allowing Cooper to examine structural similarities and individual differences simultaneously.

With rigorous coursework and alignment to undergraduate college classes, AP courses in high schools have historically been competitive and selective. However, issues of equity and access have led many school districts to remove entrance requirements to encourage more students to enroll in AP classes (Riley 2005; Schneider 2009, 831). At the same time, however, the number of students who fail AP exams is growing (Lewin 2010, A19). This creates a context in which teachers have to consider how their grades may provide assessment information to multiple audiences, and they need to potentially balance that with information produced by the AP exam results.

Teachers in this study (Cooper 2017) worked in poverty-impacted schools in which entrance requirements for AP had recently been dropped or relaxed and in which many students would be the first in their families to attend college. Teachers considered themselves "brokers" of their students' transition into college: taking their role very seriously to provide a vision of what being a college student entailed and the opportunity to experience higher education. The grades the teachers assigned became, in this context, information students could use to know if they were "college ready."

Mr. Thomas felt a duty to make sure his students were adequately prepared for college. Therefore, he called on both AP and college expectations to explain his policy of not permitting students to refine and revise their work: "Because kids need to be able to demonstrate mastery but in most colleges, they get one shot at it. I don't know that the re-testing to show mastery on the standard is appropriate in an AP course" (Cooper 2017, 28).

Ms. Nelson also believed strongly that she had to prepare her students for college. When asked if she allowed students to redo assignments and retake tests, she replied, "I've spoken to professors at [the state university] . . . and they don't allow them. I just don't want it to be a huge shock when they become freshmen" (Cooper 2017, 28). As they evaluated student work and produced summary grades, these teachers considered both practices at the local university and the AP expectations, negotiating two external contexts along with their position in a school serving students from underrepresented groups.

Teachers experienced tension as they tried to balance clear communication about college-level work with student motivation and persistence. As shown in figure 2.2, in determining first-semester final grades, teachers balanced playing the "judge" with the need to encourage ("coach") their students toward future learning opportunities—to mentor them to persist and see that they too can learn.

Four of the five teachers expressed this tension. Ms. Smith wanted to be a tough grader but worried about the meaning of the assessment artifact she was producing:

> I don't want to grade easily and give them all good grades, because . . . then they go to college and totally bomb it. The same way, I have these really high expectations because I took a lot of environmental science classes in college and this is the stuff that I had to do and this is a college-level class and they're not

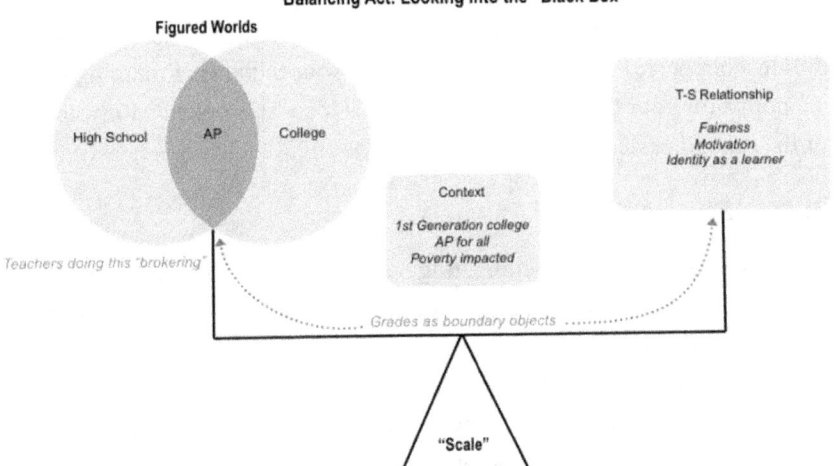

Figure 2.2 Cooper's Decision Making Structure. Cooper, Susan E. 2017. "Decisions and Tensions: Summative Assessment in PBL Advanced Placement Classes." PhD diss., University of Washington, Seattle. ProQuest (10288465), 30.

doing that. . . . Then does that A mean they really should have gotten an A? I don't know. Those are the things that weigh on me (Cooper 2017, 30).

During the semester, when earned grades prompted concerns about discouraging students, a teacher might manipulate grades by adding or modifying assessments before the end of the semester. For example, Ms. Smith worried about the affect students' grades would have on their motivation to continue in the AP course. She planned to boost students' grades by replacing the provided final exam with an easy vocabulary-matching test.

Think-aloud protocols while determining semester grades revealed teachers' in-the-moment decision-making. This example from Ms. Wall's protocol shows how teachers took other, informal observations of students' performance into account when assigning borderline grades:

> When I'm thinking about it, it's only like she randomly came up with the fact, "Hey, when I lived in Liberia, our water usage were so much lower." I'm like, "Okay, you're adding on another factor to the whole water standard. I know you are making these connections and really thinking about things." If I'm debating between a 2 and a half and a 3, then I'm like, okay probably a 3, because she's making connections. She's had experiences (Cooper 2017, 36).

She also described trying to take students' "thinking" into account when grading, to give a "boost" that would "motivate" them: "I'm not a college level teacher here. I feel your thinking, I like your thinking, I'm going to give you points for your thinking. . . . For the final a boost is better. Motivate them for the second semester" (Cooper 2017, 32).

Multiple Layers of Context

In addition to negotiating competing values between college expectations and supporting first-generation, college-bound students, each participating teacher was dealing with the change mandated by the district to move from a traditional grading system to a Standards-Referenced Grading (SRG) system.

Three of the teacher participants (Thomas, Nelson, and Wall) expressed doubt about how they could follow the tenets of SRG while maintaining the integrity of an AP course. When asked how he would handle that, Thomas replied, "I don't know yet, because one of the tenets of standard-referenced grading is that kids can retest to show mastery on a standard. Unless the colleges are doing that, which I don't think they are, I don't know how applicable [SRG] is to an AP course" (Cooper 2017, 37).

Although the five teachers graded their students quite differently despite the same curriculum, assessments, and professional development meetings, there was a structure to their decision-making. As shown in figure 2.2, all (except Ms. Nelson) alternated between using grades to communicate level of readiness for the world of college and using grades to encourage students to persist as learners and seek further opportunities to learn. While most of the teachers, at the beginning of each interview, said they produced semester grades based on collected scores, each teacher went on to demonstrate, during think-alouds, the use of other elements when giving a final summative grade.

FINAL THOUGHTS

Understanding teachers' assessment practice requires understanding the multiple contexts within which they assess. As policy makers and administrators consider ways to improve assessment in schools to promote student learning, seeing assessment as a function of an educational system is critical. Decisions made at one level of a system influence actions at other levels.

To complicate this picture further, assessments that occur in school settings are also used in other systems for different and sometimes conflicting purposes. While teachers are important players in assessment, they are not the only ones assessing or producing assessment artifacts. Efforts to improve assessment literacy need to focus not just on teachers but on all levels of the educational system.

REFLECTION QUESTIONS

1. How can states, districts, and schools emphasize use of balanced, comprehensive assessment systems like NCSAS to inform and improve teaching and learning?
2. How can districts maximize the use of all forms of professional learning—face-to-face, independent study, virtual, coaching—to promote appropriate use of classroom-based assessment to improve outcomes for every student?

NOTE

1. All names are pseudonyms.

Chapter 3

Integrate Assessment and Teaching

Cara Jackson, Scott Reed, and Kim Walters-Parker

SECTION BY CARA JACKSON

Making the most of instructional time is essential for effective, equitable teaching. Assessments can provide crucial information to guide instructional decisions in ways that best meet the needs of students. This chapter describes the research base behind integrating assessment and teaching, as well as case study examples of the application of such research in two different types of high school classrooms: physics and reading intervention.

Research Base for the Integration of Assessment and Teaching

Educators can use assessment data to inform goal setting, determine what content to teach and how to teach it, and decide what strategies to use for instruction (Tarasawa, Gotwals, and Jackson 2018). Assessment data are integrated into teaching when educators use assessments to identify student strengths and weaknesses, identify curricular topics based on students' prior knowledge and interests, determine approaches to remediation or reteaching, pace lessons, and differentiate or make grouping decisions. The sections that follow describe research on how educators have used assessments to enhance students' learning experiences.

Assessments to Plan Teaching

As noted by Penuel and Shepard (2016, 820), assessment evidence can be used to plan future learning experiences, support reflection and communication, and guide future action to improve work produced for external audiences, such as a piece of writing, an artistic performance, or a set of problems to be solved. Teachers might, for example, use assessment data to plan reteach lessons (Datnow, Park, and Kennedy-Lewis 2012, 262). The process of sensemaking around assessment can lead to different types of improvement actions, such as changes in curriculum and instruction (Schildkamp 2019, 9).

In addition to using extant assessment data to understand where students are in the learning progression, teachers should plan for the collection of evidence of student thinking throughout the lesson. Classroom activities give students the opportunity to express their thinking; feedback from teachers and peers can help develop it (Black et al. 2004, 14). The next section describes how such assessment evidence provides the basis for responsive teaching.

Assessments to Support Responsive Teaching

Assessments can help educators identify how students think about content and what instructional steps may facilitate learning. As noted in chapter 1, eliciting student thinking through questioning and examining student work can inform instructional decision-making. Well-planned questions, adequate wait time, and follow-up activities create opportunities to extend students' understanding.

Teachers need to design tasks to elicit evidence of students' understanding and use this evidence to adjust instruction to better meet the students' learning needs (Black and Wiliam 2018, 560). As Hiebert et al. (2007, 52) note, knowing what responses imply about student thinking is key to collecting evidence of students' learning and using that evidence to inform instruction.

Such integration of assessment and teaching provides the basis for promoting equity within the classroom, because teachers can use assessment data to shape their instructional practices to meet the needs of *all* students. Gathering evidence of each student's achievement of the learning goals and revising instruction based on this evidence is a first step toward greater equity (Hiebert et al. 2007, 57).

However, many teachers do not plan and conduct classroom dialogue in ways that might help all students learn (Black et al. 2004, 11). While student responses are a powerful piece of everyday data, eliciting such responses and fostering classroom discourse tends to be an area where teaching practice is weakest.

For example, Kane and Staiger (2012, 23–24) find that some of the lowest-rated practices include *instructional dialogue* on the Classroom Assessment Scoring System (CLASS) rubric, *using questioning and discussion techniques* on the Danielson Group Framework for Teaching, and *classroom discourse* on Protocol for Language Arts Teaching Observations (PLATO) Prime. Sherrington (2019, 31) contends that checks for understanding are the single biggest common area for improvement in teaching.

Determining if Teaching Was Successful

One key purpose of assessment is to know whether teaching has enabled students to reach their learning targets. "Students do not always learn what they are taught, so we need to develop processes of eliciting and interpreting evidence so that we can draw conclusions about what students have in fact learned" (Black and Wiliam 2018, 71). Similarly, Datnow, Park, and Kennedy-Lewis (2012, 259) note that the results of benchmark assessments can serve as a form of feedback to teachers regarding whether students have mastered the concepts and skills that have been taught.

As such, assessment of student learning provides information to teachers regarding the strengths and weaknesses of their instructional practices (Datnow, Park, and Kennedy-Lewis 2012, 259). While teachers may be dismayed to discover that instruction was weak in the sense that students did not learn what was taught, analyzing classroom practice and testing hypothesized improvements supports the growth of expertise (Hiebert et al. 2007, 57).

Foster Student Engagement in the Learning Process

Assessments can also be used to engage learners in their own growth, as specified in *InTASC Model Core Teaching Standards* developed by the Council of Chief State School Officers (2013, 9). Students can play an active role in setting learning goals based on past performance or desired long-term goals.

In addition, students are an important and often overlooked source of insight into their own thinking (Mintz, Fiarman, and Buffett 2006, 91). Asking students questions about their understanding can help educators understand and address student misconceptions. Finally, assessments that document progress toward goals can be used to motivate students to achieve personal bests (Wiliam and Leahy 2015, 117).

This chapter's case studies both highlight the cognitive science principles behind assessment as an integral part of teaching and describe myriad ways of using assessments to support responsive teaching. In the first case study, Scott Reed discusses how he used frequent assessment cards to improve teaching and learning opportunities in his physics classes. In the second case study, Kim Walters-Parker describes how assessment practices based on cognitive science principles can be incorporated in the classroom.

CASE STUDY BY SCOTT REED

Assessment as a Guide to Teaching

Classroom teachers recognize a need to integrate assessment with the learning opportunities within the classroom. This case study explores a strategy of integrating assessments by separating larger end-of-the-week quizzes into multiple smaller quizzes that were used throughout the week.

The classes selected for this case study were all first-year regular physics classes at a school in a Chicago suburb. All four classes comprised students in grades eleven and twelve, ranging in age from sixteen to eighteen. Approximately 15 percent of the students had identified special needs, and accommodations were provided as needed. Students in these classes were at an average-to-high math and science level, and most of the juniors took an Advanced Placement (AP) or honors science course in their senior year.

Throughout the year, the teacher experimented with giving students more frequent, but smaller and less formal, assessments that included opportunities for students to self-reflect on their understanding. Except for the end-of-unit assessments and mid-semester projects, all other assessments were broken into a smaller set of two or three questions that fit on a quarter sheet of cardstock paper (called "cards").

The teacher assigned cards daily at various times within the period, including as lesson starters, pre-lab prediction responses, mid-lesson checks for understanding, and exit slips. Sometimes the cards served as quizzes that the teacher collected for feedback with a grade assigned. Other times the cards were not graded and instead served as practice for the students to complete initially on their own and then revise as needed after discussion. For all cards, the students were encouraged to correct their work and talk it through with a classmate, school tutor, or the teacher.

Every card assessment asked students to preevaluate their understanding of the content. When students returned the cards, the teacher gave students another opportunity to self-reflect on the feedback and their shift in understanding, as well as set a goal and plan for improvement as needed. The set of cards were kept on a ring, maintained and referenced by the students throughout each unit. These cards were then reevaluated toward the end of a unit in a student-led conference with the teacher, with two final reflections by the students: "I used to believe these ideas, but now I understand these concepts," and "I still need help with these skills, and this is why."

In a given week, the students completed about ten assessment cards. A third of these were quizzes, for which the teacher gave feedback and assigned a grade. As the cards were collected, the teacher quickly assessed which students answered the quiz questions correctly or not. This information allowed the teacher to make decisions on grouping and questioning for each student, while it also provided the instructor an awareness of the pulse of the entire class. The teacher used the student preevaluation of their understanding to guide instruction as well—it gave a sense of the "speed limit" of the upcoming lesson.

The teacher did not grade the remaining cards of the week, though the cards provided vital information to both the teacher and students. These included mid-lesson check-ups for students' own progress toward the learning targets, pre-lab and post-lab applications of the performance expectations, and exit slips that challenged the students to synthesize the newly learned content with prior knowledge and skills. The nongraded cards allowed the students to reflect on their understanding, share ideas with their classmates, and make revisions to their initial responses to make them more complete.

The assessment cards were most effective when students reflected on their learning and set goals for improvement. Before the students turned in the assessment, they reflected on their understanding at the moment by marking the location on the card along a continuum from "I don't get it at all" to "I fully understand." Then they had an opportunity to share what they need more of, such as time, instruction, or practice. As the cards were collected, the teacher gained a sense of where the students thought they were individually and as a whole class. The students' collective reflections to their understanding level and what they needed to improve shaped the teacher's approach to the day.

Identifying Student Strengths and Weakness

The students' strengths and weaknesses in applying new skills and knowledge were revealed as card assessments were given throughout the school year. As the students reflected on the feedback from their peers and teacher, the students gained an awareness of the tasks and concepts that they understood well in addition to the ones that they needed more time to develop.

Students commonly reflected on questions such as "What do I still need help with specifically within a lesson or learning task?" "Is this something that is specific to this lesson or more general throughout the unit?" and "What am I going to do about it?" One of the ways the teacher made this exercise a part of their educational routine was providing time in class for students to rank their understanding before and after the card assessment and define a short-term goal for remediation as needed.

It was powerful to witness the students gain the confidence of mastery of a skill or concept. This past year, a student challenged herself by taking a more advanced physics class than she was recommended to take. Even though she received one of the lowest grades in the class, she often exhibited mastery over the concepts and skills. Knowing this allowed her to participate at a high level in small and large groups by capitalizing on the moments when she was confident. Likewise, at other times she needed help with specific concepts and skills; therefore, she could be proactive in seeking and accessing the help she needed.

Determining What to Teach

Daily small assessment cards provided more frequent checks of student understanding than larger quizzes given at the end of multiple days of instruction. These daily assessments also led to more frequent conversations with students about their understanding. As a result of using the card assessment strategy, every day the teacher gained a solid understanding of where students were with regard to the learning targets and performance expectations of the course. As misconceptions were revealed, the teacher used the data to determine what additional experiences and practice the class as a whole needed, and which individual students needed additional support to ensure equitable opportunities to master the content.

The cards revealed what to teach in two powerful ways this past year—after a reading assignment at the beginning of the week and in response to a lab experience during the middle of the week. Every weekend, the students were expected to read the content that the class would cover in the coming week.

On Monday, the students shared with each other in small groups what they had learned. Students often discussed the most challenging passages from the text and encouraged others within their team to provide feedback and assistance. The card quiz focused on the reading showed the teacher how well the students could apply the knowledge learned through reading and collaboration. Even though this was an individual quiz, the reading assessment was really the result of a team effort since the students read to help themselves while also helping their teams build a collective understanding of the content.

Every reading assessment card provided an opportunity to share and answer a question of the student's own design. The prompt was "What is something else that the teacher should have asked about the reading, and what is the answer to the question?" In reflection on this process of asking questions of their own design, students shared that challenging themselves to write their own questions inspired additional thinking instead of simply regurgitating what they read or solved the night before. It also introduced the students to more questions than the teacher would have created, which led to even more thinking.

The process helped students gain confidence and greater awareness of what they knew and did not know. Writing questions empowered the students to communicate their understanding in unique ways while increasing their accountability as well. As a result of the questions that the students included in these quizzes, the teacher adjusted the lessons that followed to incorporate the ideas shared about the reading.

After a lab, assessment cards were used to see how the students grew as a result of the lab experience. Often the lab required synthesizing and applying skills and knowledge that they had gained in previous lessons, and so a well-crafted exit assessment card allowed the teacher to monitor student improvement in understanding and skills. It also revealed what the students still needed to work on.

The instructional days that followed a lab were often differentiated as students worked on one of a number of skills in smaller groupings. These work groups were not usually sorted by their lab teams but instead by the student's individual educational needs so that students would have additional practice with a skill or concept with which they needed more help. The student data collected on the lab assessment cards determined this differentiation.

Pacing Lessons

Smaller but more frequent assessments gave the teacher a greater sense of the time needed to address different components of the lesson. In past years, when quizzes were administered solely at the end of the week, issues with comprehension were caught too late and misunderstandings compounded throughout the week. The teacher spent a substantial amount of time going over the assessments to address errors that should have been remedied earlier in the week.

By using the assessment cards instead of the end-of-the-week quizzes, the teacher had real-time data every day. This more timely information allowed the teacher to have a better sense of the time needed for the students to collectively understand the learning targets and meet the performance expectations of the lesson.

Using the system of assessment cards resulted in a weekly calendar that was more dynamic and more likely to change midweek. Students appreciated this flexibility and became more likely to admit not understanding a concept when they knew that the concept was an important part of the flow of the unit. This process was not focused on getting through the content but instead built on everyone's understanding.

The cards' versatility gave each student equitable access to the assessments because not only were the cards introduced at various learning entry points throughout the week, but they also allowed individual students to use feedback and reflection to meet their specific needs. While some students required more than the time provided in class to grasp a concept, all students left class with their needs identified so they would know what they needed to continue to work on outside of class.

Moreover, the quality of the time spent in the class shifted. Formal and informal assessment cards gave both a measure of how many students were ready to move on and an opportunity for students to reflect and identify areas of improvement to work on and areas of strength to build on. This focus made the time more efficient and individualized for each student, ensuring more equitable instruction to meet the needs of all learners.

As students became better at reflecting, they grew more willing and able to communicate their understanding and any need for clarification to the teacher. As a result, toward the end of the year the teacher was able to reduce reliance on the beginning-of-class assessment cards and instead depended on students to communicate their instructional needs.

Making Grouping Decisions to Address Educational Needs

The assessment cards used in this case study were introduced to a course in which students traditionally worked in groups, often during labs. However, the variety of groups improved due to the increase in daily information about student learning collected by the teacher and the change in the focus on students' individual learning. Homogeneous and heterogeneous groupings still had their purpose throughout the year and were often assigned using the assessment data from the cards.

The addition of reading assessment cards led to the development of reading assessment teams. Groups of three students were established within the first few weeks of the school year. The team members were responsible for reading the assigned pages from the textbook over the weekend. The reading group teams then collaborated at the beginning of the school week, helping each other understand and process the content. These groups were formed primarily by student choice and fluctuated a bit as students developed collegiality in working with each other. After group discussions as a reading team, each student took a reading quiz independently.

For all other team exercises used within the classroom, data from the assessment cards was used in the formation of groupings after the assessment. The teacher used a class starter card to group students homogeneously based on students' perceived understanding and performance on the assessment. A pre-lab card assisted in the grouping of students with similar initial plans for exploring the phenomena and their proposed lab design. A homework quiz card enabled the teacher to make heterogeneous groupings the next day for more advanced work on the concept. Altogether, the additional information collected on the students' performance on the assessments as well as their ideas and understandings led to more effective grouping strategies throughout the unit.

Setting Goals and Determining Approaches to Remediation

Student goal setting was a significant improvement over strategies used in past years. With each card, students were expected to evaluate their perceived understanding, answer the question(s), and then set learning goals after discussing the results of the card in class and while processing the teacher feedback. These goals were usually short term and actionable, such as "review the examples in the book," "watch the suggested video online," "complete additional practice at this website," "see a tutor in the tutoring center," and "come in for help with the teacher during office hours."

As the students developed a habit of setting goals, a transformation occurred. The students not only understood the content better, but they also became more aware of their own learning strengths and areas for improvement. The students took ownership of their learning in very authentic and individualized ways.

Reflection on their understanding and identifying their learning goals allowed the students to discern areas where they needed extra instruction, time, and support. By seeing reflection as an essential part of the assessment process, students were challenged to consider their understanding before the assessment and after they received feedback. Each assessment card led to more student self-awareness of their achievements and learning goals.

This process also pushed the teacher to be more proactive in meeting the educational needs of all students. When the students set goals for further practice, the teacher was able to respond to the patterns observed within the students' goals by having additional materials ready. During the times of the school year when many students needed to seek extra tutoring or support outside of class, the teacher gained additional insights regarding pacing and the need for increased scaffolding of complex ideas. As a whole, the students' goals often resulted in a recalibration of the unit goals and the plan to address the learning targets of the course.

At the end of a unit, the students were encouraged to make corrections paired with conversations with the teacher. Not only did this lead to further learning gains by the students, but it improved the teacher's approaches as well. Through the one-to-one conversations, the teacher recorded trends with each student individually and with the class. These insights impacted the approaches to future units within and beyond the school year for both the teacher and the students.

A student this past year took this exercise a step further and used the card as a reminder of her goals. She kept the cards she still needed help with paper-clipped in her assignment notebook and did not remove them until she achieved her learning goals. She quickly learned how to structure a system of remediation and reteaching that was personalized to her specific needs. As the year progressed, she modified her system of self-reflection and goal setting to be independent of the card. The structure and routine of this more frequent assessment, reflection, and feedback led her to develop a life skill that she now can apply in any class or setting.

The teacher was involved in this evaluation process as well. The student reflection continuum gave a quick view during the lesson of the perceived understanding of each student and therefore the class as a whole. The teacher made instructional decisions in real time during the day's lessons to address any gaps in the students' perceived understanding.

Although perceived understanding was not the complete representation of what the students had learned, it guided the teacher during the instruction for the day. It gave helpful clues to the teacher as to whether to slow down to reteach a concept to the entire class by incorporating it within the day's lesson or to provide a more differentiated approach in the coming days to just a few students that needed to get back on track.

Supporting the Educational Needs of Students

Even though the total number of "quiz questions" was essentially the same when comparing the old assessment model with the new assessment card strategy, student responsiveness to the assessment data was greatly improved. The students became advocates for their own learning and were less likely to fall so far behind that they could not keep up on their own.

They used learning supports at a higher rate. The schoolwide tutoring center experienced an increase in scheduled appointments from the teacher's classes (both drop-in and routinely scheduled ones), and student study groups organically developed and thrived throughout the year. Students were also more likely to seek help from their teacher, and these tutoring sessions started with a more positive focus—from "I don't get this at all, and I am totally lost" to "I have a quick question that I hope can get me back on track."

The teacher became more responsive to the students' collective and individual needs as well. The processes of creating assessments and using the assessment data were informed by the teacher's understanding of individual students, and this in turn supported more equitable teaching and learning. Small adjustments to the weekly schedule and individual lessons eliminated the need to make major adjustments after a comprehensive quiz with mixed results. These whole-group adjustments, along with individualized supports based on student-specific needs, created the learning opportunities needed to ensure equitable access to the course material.

Throughout the year, quiz questions underwent a transformation. Questions became less focused on recall, with a greater emphasis on the students using and applying what they learned. Problems that required finding the right equation and plugging in the right numbers were replaced with ranking tasks that required less calculator math and a more advanced understanding of the relationship between the variables.

A few short-answer questions were replaced by a single prompt that required a more thorough written response. In some situations, students were asked to authentically design a lab and complete it, and then they used the card to reflect on their work or transfer their new understanding to a novel situation.

The process of student reflection on each card also fostered students' thinking about what they needed to do to improve their understanding. After a few months of reflection, the students commonly asked questions like "I see that I need more practice; what can I do?" or "Extra problems aren't going to help until I understand this concept; do you have time to go over this with me?" The students became better self-advocates because they better understood their gaps in understanding and what steps would likely result in the necessary growth. Learning new content and skills became much less daunting for the students and the teacher when they were addressed in smaller pieces.

Celebrating Successes

By splitting up a period-long weekly quiz into ten smaller quiz-like experiences throughout the week, the students and teacher experienced positive gains. Hallmarks of the card assessments included more reflection before and after the assessment, more teamwork and a greater variety of teams, more individualized instruction, and more student ownership of the learning process. In addition, students also achieved better performance on summative exams, especially on the questions that required higher-order processing.

As the shift was made to more formative assessments, the teacher's instruction shifted as well, with less "gearing up" for the few big assessments and more opportunities to think critically about the content, synthesize ideas, and apply understandings in authentic ways.

For example, in the past, the teacher might have designed a lab to instill one key idea that the students would see on a quiz, but now lab work became an opportunity to celebrate the diverse thinking and approaches from the students. In such an approach to lab work, the same phenomena were explored in different ways, and those ideas were communicated. In this way with the labs and many other educational experiences throughout the week, the card assessment provided flexibility and responsiveness that gave the students more choices, greater insights into their own understandings, and greater ownership of their learning.

CASE STUDY BY KIM WALTERS-PARKER

The Case for Assessment as Teaching

"Is that what *my* brain looks like? No, for real, is it?"
"Why do you have a brain in a reading class? Doesn't that belong in a science class?"

Excellent questions. Why would a high school reading specialist teaching reading intervention classes have a model of a human brain in her classroom? Besides the fact that a realistic model of a human brain is inherently interesting to kids, reading and learning occur in the brain. The model is a concrete representation of the brain's components that must coordinate their functions for reading, learning, and other cognitive processes to work. Experience has demonstrated that the better students understand how they read and learn, the better they can manage their own reading and learning.

Given the likelihood that a high school reading intervention class will be the last opportunity many students have to develop their reading and learning skills, every opportunity to promote that development is precious. Strategies are included in the curriculum based on their portability and practicality outside the immediate classroom setting, whether in a postsecondary, workplace, or military context, or even in a student's personal life.

Every class period has a sense of urgency. That sense of urgency led to the adoption of assessment practices that leverage principles of cognitive psychology to go beyond assessment *of* learning, assessment *for* learning, and even assessment *as* learning. These practices leverage principles of cognitive psychology for assessment *as teaching.*

Cognitive Psychology in the Classroom

Cognitive psychology, loosely defined as the scientific study of the mind and its processes, plays a major role in how these reading intervention classes are structured. Reading is explicitly modeled and practiced as a cognitive process around which particular strategies are organized.

For example, a prereading strategy would be taught not just as a procedure to do before reading but as one option among many that can accomplish the goals of prereading, particularly activation of prior knowledge or, in the absence of prior knowledge, becoming aware that prior knowledge is weak or nonexistent. The overarching instructional goal of this approach to reading strategy instruction is for students to learn when, how, and why to implement strategies independently in support of their own reading and learning.

Empowering students to enact these strategies independently supports equitable learning opportunities for students. Such strategies may be especially critical as students progress beyond the prekindergarten through twelfth-grade school setting, given that instructional scaffolding may be minimal or absent in postsecondary institutions and workplaces. Teaching students to manage their own learning effectively supports their ability to master content independently. Enabling students to recognize when particular strategies are appropriate, how to adjust strategies to suit specific tasks, and to monitor strategies' effectiveness supports equitable outcomes.

Principles of cognitive psychology also shape the role of assessment and assessment practices in these reading classes. To achieve the instructional goals, teachers must collect and respond to assessment information. Assessment as teaching leverages principles of cognitive psychology to let the teacher collect needed information while student learning continues.

The Testing Effect

Also known as test-enhanced learning or simply retrieval practice, the testing effect occurs when retrieval in an assessment context improves subsequent recall. Decades of research in educational psychology find that the testing effect reflects a fundamental principle of cognitive psychology: consolidation of memory. Consolidation, a cognitive process that could be described informally as akin to newly learned information "sinking in," is fundamental to learning and long-term memory. Nungester and Duchastel (1982, 18) explicitly link consolidation and assessment:

> Administering quizzes to students in class is generally considered to fulfill two functions: to motivate students to study and to determine how well they have mastered the material that was taught. A third function, more directly related to the learning process, goes largely unrecognized: to help the student consolidate in memory what was learned.

The authors present experimental evidence to support the legitimacy of the test effect and conditions under which testing can best promote consolidation of memory. A deeper understanding of this type of research can help educators leverage this knowledge for more efficient instruction through assessment as teaching.

At least three of the testing effect's nuances can be explained with principles of cognitive psychology. First, the testing effect is stronger when the learner has to generate or actively retrieve rather than just recognize the information. This information can help teachers and students select item formats, perhaps including a manageable number of short-answer questions with multiple-choice items. Second, the testing effect is stronger when the learner receives feedback on the quality of answers. Recalling information incorrectly does not help with later recall of correct information, so a checking system is essential. Third, the benefits of the testing effect are more pronounced for long-term recall than for short-term recall.

Focusing on long-term recall for bell ringers (i.e., opening activities that focus on content that students have previously learned) or quiz items mixed in with newer information can help students prepare for an eventual comprehensive exam. For multiple-choice items, including distractors that draw on both long- and short-term recall can be an effective strategy. These examples demonstrate that with an even slightly deeper understanding of how the cognitive processes work, teachers and their students can transform a one-off activity or routine quiz into an effective independent learning practice.

Distributed Practice

Strategic retrieval practice schedules tend to focus on distributed practice. The testing effect demonstrates that retrieving information from memory promotes consolidation of that information in long-term memory. Information already consolidated in long-term memory can be recalled to the short-term memory and then further consolidated; revisiting information strengthens the memory, which tends to make subsequent efforts to recall that information more effective.

Retrieval practice can take many forms and can be carried out on a variety of schedules. Distributing the episodes of retrieval practice over time can lead to better retention of information and improve the chances of successful recall from long-term memory.

Also known as spaced practice, distributed practice models build on studies of retention and the decay of memory (Ebbinghaus 1964). Ebbinghaus determined that repetitions over time (distributed practice) were more effective than the same number of repetitions occurring all at once (massed practice) as a way to promote long-term retention of information and increase the likelihood that information could be recalled.

Although Ebbinghaus carried out these studies with nonsense syllables with only himself as a subject, his conclusions have been supported by thousands of subsequent studies and have been shown to hold true for memory in general, not just memory of nonsense syllables. Considered in the context of assessment in particular, understanding that distributed practice is more effective than massed practice can help teachers develop instructional schedules that support student learning and help students manage their own learning more efficiently.

Teachers and students need to know only a few basic concepts to leverage distributed practice. In the reading intervention classes described earlier, teachers model distributed practice not only by explicitly explaining it but also by embedding it in the design of the lesson as well. Distributed practice influences instructional pacing and strategically scheduled repetition.

Students who incorporate distributed practice in their studying are less likely to end up cramming for tests at the last minute. The time span over which repetitions are most effectively distributed may vary by person and context. Although classic studies of distributed practice often operationalize delay between repetitions in terms of days, scheduling of classes (such as meeting on alternate days) may prevent teachers from ensuring that students will be able to engage in repetition at specific times.

As a form of modeling, the teacher routinely introduces new information at the beginning of a 90-minute block, provides time for practice, and revisits the information at the end of the block as part of a classic closure process.

That information is typically revisited early in the next class to bring it back from long-term memory and then again later in the class. At that point, the rehearsals are typically spaced further and further apart.

This kind of process is done very intentionally and very transparently, so the students understand why they are hearing the same thing more than once. If a student complains, "You already said that," the teacher and the other students are reminded that realizing the information is being repeated means the distributed practice is working. This offers a good opportunity to have a student recall information independently rather than just recognize it, taking advantage of another principle of cognitive psychology and modeling the type of recall that will most likely be needed for an assessment, formative or summative.

Dual Coding

Dual coding theory suggests that information stored in memory may be encoded in what amounts to a verbal format, an image format, or both verbal and image formats (Paivio 1969, 241). Because this informal explanation of dual coding may sound similar to learning styles, it is important to distinguish between the two. Learning styles theory is generally associated with a position that individuals have a modality (visual, auditory, tactile, and kinesthetic) through which they learn best. Learning styles theory is sometimes considered a means of individualizing instruction, but researchers have found no evidence to indicate that tailoring instruction to students' learning styles improves learning (Pashler et al. 2009, 105). Dual coding, on the other hand, is supported by a solid research base rooted in cognitive psychology.

Classroom applications of dual coding theory focus on including multiple representations of information when possible and extend to both instruction and assessment. For example, whenever possible, texts with graphics that support content are favored over texts without supporting graphics for use in the developmental reading classes. Images that serve mostly as decoration actually create a distraction for readers; thus, students are taught to evaluate whether they should revisit those images or ignore them. The teacher models note-taking strategies that involve not only words but also pictures, drawings, maps, and other graphic representations, and a gradual release of responsibility ensures that students develop portable skills for independent application.

Some material seems ideal for this approach: photosynthesis can be explained in words and represented in images quite easily. An abstract concept like independence seems more fit for words than images, but the effort to create a suitable image may require the student to process the information longer, which should actually result in more effective consolidation. Dual coding theory suggests that reviewing both formats would create a stronger and more easily retrieved memory than one format or the other.

Dual coding theory can also inform assessment practices. Assessment items can include both words and images, and teachers can give students flexibility in response formats when feasible. Again, drawing an image to demonstrate understanding of photosynthesis may be more natural than drawing an image to demonstrate understanding of independence, but both tasks reflect an opportunity for students to benefit from applications of dual coding in the classroom.

When flexibility is not feasible, students can be coached to plan their answers by activating both the words and the images they have studied. That is the case with standardized end-of-course exams students might take at the end of a high school class, common exams in college class, or licensing tests at the end of a training program. If students have studied using both types of representations, the chances that they will recall important information are maximized because there are effectively two pathways by which learners can retrieve information from their long-term memory.

Implications

Assessment as teaching is a powerful concept that involves applying principles of cognitive psychology in tandem with classroom assessment practices. These efforts are intentional and transparent, explained to students so they develop portable learning strategies that they can apply in novel contexts. Students who know how to use effective learning strategies and understand how and why the strategies work are empowered as learners. This model supports goals of education in general and intervention in particular.

Broadening the application of assessment as teaching would not be particularly time-consuming or burdensome. Perhaps the biggest hurdle to broader implementation is teacher capacity, which typically hinges on either in-service professional development or preservice educator preparation. Until capacity is developed through those avenues, interested educators can collaborate with other professionals to implement assessment as teaching practices using credible online sources and materials. Chapter 6 explores the advantages of such collaboration in more detail.

REFLECTION QUESTIONS

1. Assessment cards built on and improved students' self-reflection and goal-setting skills. What additional training might be useful for the students and teacher at the beginning of the year before starting this process?
2. In what ways could technology be used to improve the card assessment strategy?
3. Which assessment as teaching practices do you already use or would you like to try?
4. How can students be taught to apply those practices independently?
5. What principles of cognitive psychology do students need to understand to be able to use that practice independently?

Chapter 4

Clarify Learning Targets

Amelia Wenk Gotwals, Dee Fabry, and Marc LaCelle-Peterson

SECTION BY AMELIA WENK GOTWALS

Imagine how confusing it would be to play a game if there were no indications for how to win or how frustrating it would be to try to drive to a party if the invitation did not include where the party was taking place. Without having a clear vision of the end goal, it is very difficult to make meaningful progress.

This rule holds true in the classroom as well. Teachers and learners need to know what they are trying to accomplish. By understanding the end goal, teachers and learners can evaluate whether they have met the target. If they have not met the target, they can figure out which steps they must take to get there. This chapter describes the research base behind the use of learning targets to support learning, as well as a case study example of the application of such research in an online master's program with a specialization in assessment literacy.

Learning targets can be defined as "statement[s] of what students are expected to demonstrate as a result of instructional activity" (Randel and Clark 2013, 147) and include the "process of establishing a direction for learning" (Marzano, Pickering, and Pollock 2001, 93). The importance of learning targets is recognized in research and observational frameworks developed for teacher evaluation in the United States and internationally (see Martinez, Taut, and Schaaf 2016, 22). For example, the Danielson Framework (Danielson 2013, 27–29) and The Observational Protocol Based on the

Art and Science of Teaching (Marzano 2010) each list learning targets as a key element of effective instruction.

The universal recognition of the importance of learning targets may be because clear learning targets allow teachers and students to align instruction, assessment, and feedback toward a common learning outcome. Aligning these features can improve coherence in the learning process (Wiggins and McTighe 2005, 15).

Effective learning targets are clear, aligned to standards, and explicit about the criteria needed to meet those standards (Randel and Clarke 2013, 147). In addition, when constructing learning targets, it is important to connect them to students' lived experiences and to make sure that they represent rigorous and core learning in the discipline. Marzano, Pickering, and Pollock (2001, 95) suggest that effective learning targets should describe three things:

- performance expectations for students;
- the conditions under which the learning will occur;
- a clearly defined threshold for mastery.

Furthermore, learning targets should be understandable and written in a way that makes sense to students. Often, learning targets are paired with rubrics or other tools that help illustrate what a road to success may look like (Arter and McTighte 2001, 46).

In addition to having high-quality learning targets, teachers must find ways of ensuring students understand the learning targets. Without clearly communicated learning targets, teachers and students may not have the same vision for what is to be learned. These differing visions for learning may cause confusion for students in terms of why they are doing certain activities. In addition, without a shared vision, students may not know how to best represent their understandings.

Huinker and Freckmann (2009, 7–9) argue that effective teacher implementation of learning goals includes four characteristics:

- First, before instruction, the teacher develops a clear and communicable goal of the concepts that students will learn.
- Second, teachers translate this goal into student-friendly language.
- Third, students describe the concepts they will be learning or are currently learning.

- Finally, teachers articulate the alignment of their lesson progression with district, state, and national standards for learning.

Learning targets can also support students in self-assessing their progress (Allal 2010, 350, vol. 3). When students understand the goals for learning, they are better able to evaluate the quality of their own and their peer's work (Roth et al. 2011, 140). When teachers share learning expectations verbally or through rubrics and involve students in the construction of learning goals, instruction tends to become more student-centered, and students are more likely to take responsibility for their own work (Andrade, Du, and Wang 2008, 10).

Overall, clear learning targets are a cornerstone to effective assessment and instruction. By having a clear target, teachers can structure activities to support student learning. Having a clear end goal allows students to be metacognitive about where they are in their learning process and take ownership of their learning.

This chapter's case study presents information about a master's level course focused on creating clear learning targets. Dr. Dee Fabry and Dr. Marc LaCelle-Peterson describe how and why they designed the components of this course in the ways that they did. They also provide examples of how students worked through the course, suggesting that even experienced teachers may enjoy and benefit from examining ways in which learning targets can be used to support teaching and learning.

CASE STUDY BY DEE FABRY AND MARK LACELLE-PETERSON

An Assessment Literacy Course— Creating Clear Learning Targets

This case study includes practicing teachers who participated in a master's level course within a research-based, practice-oriented master's program with a four-course specialization in assessment literacy.

It all began when a College of Education dean charged her teacher education co-chairs and faculty with designing, developing, and implementing an innovative curriculum that would engage teachers and their students in transformative learning. A new master's degree emerged with three specializations.

This chapter focuses on the Advanced Assessment Literacy Specialization, and highlights the second course in the specialization, Creating Clear Learning Targets, which two of the authors co-developed and taught. See textbox 4.1 (at the end of the chapter) for the course outline. Throughout this study the authors refer to the teachers enrolled in the program as either *teachers* or *candidates*. The reference to *students* means the teacher's or candidate's K-12 classroom learners.

TEXTBOX 4.1   CREATING CLEAR LEARNING TARGETS COURSE OUTLINE

Topic 1. Identify learning targets that will be the focus of instruction and assessment

Inquiry self-assessment guiding questions:

- How are clear learning targets essential to sound assessment?
- What are the benefits of clear learning targets to teachers, students, and parents?

Student Learning Outcomes

    2A. Identify the five types of learning targets and when to address each. Program Learning Outcome (PLO) 2, InTASC Standard 6.
    2B. Understand the benefits and impact of clear learning targets to teachers, students, and parents. PLO 2, InTASC Standard 6.

Materials: Chappuis, Jan, Rick Stiggins, Steve Chappuis, and Judith Arter, J. 2012. *Classroom Assessment for Student Learning: Doing It Right—Using It Well*. 2nd ed. Upper Saddle River, NJ: Pearson.

Invitation for learning and sharing: Join us to discuss who gains when we set clear learning targets and how we can use this information to change teaching and learning.

Join the blog *Types of Learning Targets*: Follow the directions to create a blog post on the types of learning targets. How does knowing the five types of learning targets increase your skills as an inspired teacher? How might this knowledge impact your students' learning?

Assignment: Create a presentation on the topic "Clear Learning Targets for Student Success." The target audience for this presentation is the family that supports your students.

Topic 2. Designing assessments that align with clear learning targets

Inquiry Self-Assessment Guiding Questions

- What are the four basic categories of assessment methods?
- How can this knowledge help me as a classroom teacher?
- What is the relationship between these assessment methods and clear learning targets?

Student Learning Outcomes

2C. Differentiate the different kinds of and purposes for formative assessment methods. PLO 3; InTASC Standard 6.

2D. Match the five kinds of targets to the different formative assessment methods to create student learning opportunities. PLO 2; InTASC Standard 6.

We will be introduced to the four assessment methods; determine how to choose which method to use for any given learning target; and talk about planning and development.

Student Learning Outcome

2D. Match the five kinds of targets to the different formative assessment methods to create student learning opportunities. PLO 2; InTASC Standard 6.

Materials: Readings, videos, and articles

Invitation for sharing and learning: Join us to discuss the four basic categories of assessment and to answer, "How can I use this information?"

Assignment: Matching Methods to Targets to Learning Targets

Directions: There are two options for this assignment. Select the one you find most appropriate to your teaching.

Option A

Return to the week one assignment, "Classifying Learning Targets." You were asked to describe how the learning targets for the unit were assessed. (6. How are the learning targets currently assessed?)

Using the information from "Matching Assessment Methods to Learning Targets," analyze if the assessments you identified are the most appropriate. If they are not, select the most appropriate assessment method to use for each target. Discuss how the changes will impact your teaching and student learning.

Option B

Practice with Target-Method Match

After reading the section, "Matching Assessment Methods to Learning Targets," work independently, with a partner, or with your learning team to carry out this activity.

1. Select a short unit that you are currently teaching or will teach this year.
2. List the learning targets that will be the focus of the unit.
3. Classify each target as knowledge, reasoning, skills, or product.
4. Using the information from "Matching Assessment Methods to Learning Targets," determine which assessment method to use for each. Present this information in a format that can be shared with colleagues.

Topic 3. Taking a Deeper Dive into Assessment Planning and Design

Inquiry Self-Assessment Questions

- What is a test blueprint? What is the purpose of a test blueprint?
- How does creating a test blueprint impact teaching and learning?

Student Learning Outcomes

2B. Understand the benefits of clear learning targets to teachers, students, and parents. PLO 2, InTASC Standard 6.

2E. Select and create formative tools for use in the classroom. PLO 2; InTASC Standard 6.

Materials: Readings, YouTube Videos

Invitation for sharing and learning: Join us to discuss your thinking on Dylan Wiliam's "Unpacking Formative Assessment" YouTube talk and to answer, "How do (or will) I apply the five strategies he presents?"

Discussion board: Share two ideas for how you can apply the five strategies for smart formative assessment.

Assignment: Assessment Development Cycle

Make a Test Blueprint

Directions: Refresh your memory on the book *Assessment Development Cycle in Classroom Assessment for Student Learning*.

Complete this activity independently, with a partner, or as a team.

1. Select a short unit that you are currently teaching or will teach this year.
2. List the major learning targets that will be the focus of the unit. Be clear about the classification of each target (knowledge, reasoning, skill, product, or disposition).
3. Select or modify one of the test blueprints in chapter 4. Write your learning targets on the test blueprint.
4. If the learning targets will be assessed with multiple assessment methods, identify which methods you will use for each target.
5. Determine the relative importance of each target (the weight it will receive) and add that information to the test blueprint form.
6. If a test for the unit already exists, compare its content to the specifications in your test blueprint. Are there any discrepancies? Describe them.
7. Revise either the test blueprint or the test itself to accurately reflect achievement on the learning targets as needed.

Assignment Field Experience: Activity 4.6. Try an Assessment for Learning Application

Directions for the field experience: After reading the section, "Assessment for Learning Using Assessment Blueprints," work independently, with a partner, or with your learning team to carry out this activity.

1. Select a unit that you are currently teaching or will be teaching this year.
2. Create a test blueprint for the unit, following the instructions in the assignment you completed this week.
3. Choose one or more of the ideas described in the section, "Assessment for Learning Using Test Blueprints." Try the idea(s) with your students.
4. Briefly describe what you did selecting the format of your choice (e.g., a written report, a video, a podcast). Include the effect the activity had on student learning.

Topic 4. Connecting the Dots

Inquiry Guiding Questions

- How do day-to-day classroom assessments either build or destroy students' confidence to learn?
- What are the impacts to socio-emotional learning of our current assessment practices?
- What do we do with this information?
- What does good feedback look like from the learners' perspective?
- How can we deliver effective, helpful, and meaningful feedback to improve student learning while promoting good socio-emotional health?

In Topic 4 we ask some hard questions. Have you considered the impact of assessments and testing on the socio-emotional literacy of your learners? Are we building or destroying student confidence in them as learners with the type and way we provide feedback? As Rick Stiggins (2014, 21) states, "The mere act of judging student achievement and communicating test results can, if not skillfully and sensitively handled, trigger emotional dynamics within learners that stop them in their tracks, literally driving them from school." Let's consider the implications of how we communicate feedback.

Student Learning Outcomes

2G. Consider the impact of assessment and testing on the social-emotional development of students. PLO 4; InTASC 6

Materials: Readings, YouTube video, TED Talk video

Discussion board: The student viewpoint concerning testing and assessment is often disregarded. Rick Stiggins shares his own struggles as a learner in this week's video and in chapter 3 of *Revolutionize Assessment*. What do your own students say about testing and assessment? How does it impact their learning?

Invitation for sharing and learning: What have you learned this week about the socio-emotional impact of assessing and testing? How can use this knowledge to change the culture of assessment in your own classroom?

Assignment: Social-Emotional Impact of Testing

Reflect on the information in both the video and chapter 3 of *Revolutionize Assessment*. How does this information connect with your own schooling experiences and your own classroom teaching? Address the idea that the student's emotional reaction to results will determine what that student does in response. Will they be challenged to do better? Will they shut down because they have just been told they cannot learn? How can we deliver effective, helpful, and meaningful feedback to improve student learning while promoting good socio-emotional health? What is your plan for creating a culture of confidence in learning? Be specific in sharing how you will take steps to instill a confidence in learning by creating clear learning targets. Apply the concepts you have learned in this course to your plan.

Assignment: Select an assignment you currently use. After you have written the clear learning targets for the assignment, decide on what kind of feedback you will provide to the learner. When will you give this feedback? In what form will the feedback be given? How will you allow for dialogue with the learner about the feedback? Keep these two inquiry questions in mind:

- What does good feedback look like from the learners' perspective?
- How can we deliver effective, helpful, and meaningful feedback to improve student learning while promoting good socio-emotional health?

One of the characteristics key to successful balanced assessment is to understand the importance of beginning assessment with a clear purpose, starting with clear and specific learning targets. In this course, the focus is on gaining knowledge, skills, and expertise to increase assessment literacy in formative assessment and setting clear learning targets. Just as a Global Position System (GPS) cannot effectively direct you to your target if the data coordinates are not accurate, your students cannot gain new knowledge if the learning targets are not clear and specific. Creating Clear Targets was designed to provide classroom teachers with a GPS to support teaching and learning.

Course Readings

Chappuis, Jan. 2015. *Seven Strategises of Assessment for Student Learning*. 2nd ed. Upper Saddle Ridge, NJ: Pearson.

Chappuis, Jan, Rick Stiggins, Steve Chappius, and Judith A. Arter. 2012. *Classroom Assessment for Student Learning: Doing It Right—Using It Well*. 2nd ed. Upper Saddle Ridge, NJ: Pearson.

Stiggins, Rick. 2014. *Revolutionize Assessment*. Thousand Oaks, CA: Corwin.

Assessment done well has the potential to influence both teaching practice and student learning (Stiggins 2017, 8). Teachers and administrators report that assessment knowledge, skills, and competencies support student learning, but teachers need additional training to use assessment data to inform instruction (Gallup and Northwest Evaluation Association 2016, 2). Consequently, the Assessment Literacy Specialization was designed to provide teachers with essential assessment knowledge, skills, and competencies.

Moreover, beyond ensuring that participating teachers had the command of the basics, the Specialization aimed to position them as experts and leaders in assessment for their schools and districts.

The entire sequence includes these four courses:

1. Purposeful Assessment;
2. Creating Clear Learning Targets;
3. Quality Assessment for Student Learning;
4. Assessment for Learning.

This master's specialization was designed so that practitioners can directly implement the knowledge and skills that they learn. The theoretical underpinnings of Universal Design for Learning are foundational, and the faculty teaching this program are expected to model the major principles: multiple means of engagement, multiple means of representation, and multiple means of expression.

The second course within the specialization, Creating Clear Learning Targets, was designed and developed with collaborative input from Dr. Rick Stiggins and is based on current research on effective assessment for, and of, learning and a data-informed approach to balanced assessment (Black and Wiliam 1998a, 1998b; Hattie and Timperley 2007; Heritage 2013; Popham 2008; Stiggins 2017). This case study explains the design and implementation of that course.

The Clear Learning Targets course helps candidates gain a deeper understanding of learning targets themselves and the relationship between particular types of learning targets and assessment techniques and strategies. The materials and assignments guide them in developing and refining instructional and assessment practices in their own teaching contexts. Candidates identify, design, and create clear learning targets to determine the assessment methods to be used. One aspect of clarity on the part of the candidates is the nature of the target—for example, whether a particular target aims at knowledge, and if so, what kind of knowledge is demanded.

Candidates select and create formative assessment tools for ongoing continuous improvement and learn how to interpret and apply data analysis to support student learning. Thus, to be successful in teaching this program, the faculty must interact meaningfully with candidates to offer them multiple ways to engage in the learning environment, to self-assess and self-reflect for the purpose of improving their practice, to share their thinking, to construct new knowledge, and to communicate through a variety of opportunities. Candidates have various options for completing assignments throughout the program and within each course.

Alignment of the Learning Targets within and across Standards

One of the key learnings in the course is to help teachers understand the interrelationship between levels of learning targets. Classroom student learning targets emerge from and align to the standards chosen by each state. Creating an alignment matrix and populating it with aligned learning targets directly correlates to learning activities and assessments and creates a more balanced approach to teaching and learning (see table 4.1). Therefore, the learning targets for the course themselves are aligned at the program, course, and candidate levels and to the Interstate Teacher Assessment and Support Consortium (InTASC) Standards (https://www.ccsso.org), specifically Standard 6: Assessment. The InTASC Standards are used by the institution to provide evidence of meeting the Council for the Accreditation of Educator Programs (CAEP) criteria.

During the course teachers consistently return to this chart to reflect on their acquisition and implementation of the learning targets. This repetition helps them gain new insights into how to connect the learning targets for their own learners.

Clear Learning Targets' Scope and Sequence and Learning Activities

The design of the specialization and the courses within it were developmentally sequenced to build new knowledge and to allow teachers time to acquire a new skill, practice it in their own classroom, reflect on the learning, and revise the learning activity. Each section of the course begins with a set of guiding questions aligned to the learning target(s). The assignments, assessments, peer interactions, and activities are all focused on the section topics.

The horizontal and vertical integration were purposefully created for continuity within and across the program. Throughout the sequence of courses, students build a balanced assessment plan that includes the following:

1. a definition of assessment literacy;
2. a personal assessment literacy philosophy;
3. characteristics of an assessment-literate education;
4. the intricacies of assessment *of* learning;
5. aspects and application of assessment *for* learning;
6. a gap analysis of their own practices;
7. a formative action plan;
8. a student/parent communication plan and strategy.

In each course the candidates build a piece of their personal master plan.

The course proceeds through three main intellectual moves, beginning with classifying learning, proceeding to matching appropriate assessments to the various types of learning targets, and concluding with the development of

Table 4.1 Alignment Matrix for Clear Learning Targets Course Chart 1

Program Learning Targets (for Masters of Science in Advanced Teaching Practices)	Assessment Literacy Specialization Learning Targets	Creating Clear Learning Targets Course Learning Targets	InTASC Standard(s)
1. Develop a personal, *inspired* educational philosophy that is grounded in historical/current practices and professional ethics to include a pathway for continuous growth.	1. Develop a personal assessment literacy philosophy that is grounded in research and professional ethics.		Standard 6: Assessment
2. Integrate increasingly sophisticated instruction, assessment, and digital learning skills for research, curriculum design, and professional growth.	2. Identify and create clear learning targets in order to align quality assessments for learning.	2A. Identify the five types of learning targets and when to address each. 2B. Explain the benefits of clear learning targets to teachers, students, and parents. 2D. Match the five kinds of targets to the different formative assessment methods to create student learning opportunities. 2E. Select and create formative tools for use in the classroom.	Standard 6: Assessment
3. Design inspired student learning experiences that include the principles of differentiated instruction, diversity, and social justice.	3. Evaluate assessments to determine appropriate implementation for student learning.	2C. Differentiate the kinds of, and purposes for, formative assessment methods.	Standard 6: Assessment

(Continued)

Table 4.1 Alignment Matrix for Clear Learning Targets Course Chart 1 *(Continued)*

Program Learning Targets (for Masters of Science in Advanced Teaching Practices)	Assessment Literacy Specialization Learning Targets	Creating Clear Learning Targets Course Learning Targets	InTASC Standard(s)
4. Apply research-based knowledge and skills to create/transform effective, diverse learning environments.	4. Create a balanced assessment plan that reflects knowledge of assessment literacy and can be used by others to improve student learning and achievement based on the assessment standards, knowledge, and skills gained in this specialization to impact teaching and learning.	2F. Implement formative assessments, interpret the data findings, and apply the information to ongoing continuous student improvement. 2G. Consider the impact of assessment and testing on the social-emotional development of students.	Standard 6: Assessment

a test blueprint that pulls together an appropriate mix of targets and assessments to guide and evaluate larger learning segments. Along the way, engaging students (and their families and caregivers) in guiding and gauging their own learning is emphasized.

Teacher Responses to Classifying Learning Targets

Classifying learning targets is the first main topic of the course. Recall that the candidates in the program are practicing teachers. In the two dozen course sections the authors have taught in the program over the past three years, candidates taking the course hold teaching assignments that range from kindergarten through high school, across all content subject areas, with years of classroom experience ranging from two to twenty-five. Regardless of level, subject, or seniority, teachers find the segment on classifying learning targets fresh and valuable.

One of the first tasks for the candidates is analyzing learning targets or objectives that they have been using in their classrooms according to the type of intellectual activity that is demanded. They then look at the set of learning targets for a unit or larger segment of instruction, analyzing each target. This exercise gives candidates an awareness of where the unit's intellectual center of gravity lies. Candidates base their work on the framework presented in Chappuis et al. (2012, 43–57), which delineates five types of learning targets:

- knowledge;
- reasoning;
- skill;
- product;
- disposition.

Finally, candidates consider the degree to which the learning targets are explained in a student-friendly language.

Candidates' work and discussion-board posts about their work often reveal interesting information about their practice. Recall that the candidates are practicing classroom teachers who have chosen to pursue graduate study—some of them long tenured and in leadership positions within their schools. Despite the fact that each of them has based instruction on objectives or learning targets they have written themselves or adopted from prepared curricula and have generally posted learning objectives in their classrooms for years, most of them find the activity of classifying learning targets by analyzing them individually and across a unit to be eye-opening and, in some cases, transformative.

For example, one candidate observed in a discussion-board post:

> I've been learning to be more intentional with the way that I approach writing and using learning targets. . . . I used to write learning targets just to have them on my board and check that off of my long to-do list of everyday tasks. They were not being used in a meaningful way where I refer to them and use them to drive my assessments. . . . The learning targets that I had were broad and maybe not specific enough. . . . I struggled classifying them as a specific type of learning target.

Another candidate responded, "I can certainly relate to your [instructor] use of learning targets early on in my career. We're asked to do so many things and pulled in so many different directions that I definitely felt like it was just another chore to complete."

These comments are typical of candidate reflections. Many candidates reported that the task of analyzing individual learning targets and groups of learning targets made them aware that, though they routinely posted learning targets, the routine was without significant impact other than as a general announcement of the topic and place-finder in relation to the larger standards-based curriculum. As another teacher put it, "I used to use learning targets as a way to introduce the content. My learning targets were used more as a 'heads up,' rather than a guide for students to check their process and work towards a goal."

For the targets to serve as "a guide for students," students need to comprehend them. Candidates were also asked to decide whether the learning targets for the unit were expressed in learner-friendly language and to revise them as needed. While roughly a fifth of the teachers in the program judged their learning targets to be stated in such a way that learners could understand them readily, the majority saw the need to alter the phrasing of the targets so that students could indeed use them as a guide to learning.

In her self-reflection, one candidate noted that because she had not previously understood the significance and impact of writing clear learning targets, the classification process was a challenge. Internalizing it was difficult for her: "I struggled classifying them as a specific type of learning target. This then made it challenging to choose a specific assessment that would [be] most appropriate for the learning target."

One candidate who had connected clear learning targets to the correct type of assessment method wrote, "I had long targets that weren't really student friendly. I'm excited as well to actually be able to create assessments that actually measure what I'd like my students to achieve."

One discussion prompt posed to several groups of candidates asked why this way of approaching learning targets rendered the targets more relevant, and whether the same impact could have been achieved earlier in their careers, specifically, in their preparation. Responses varied but generally pointed toward a need for experience with curricula as a prerequisite for engaging in deeper analysis.

As teachers gain iterative experience with a particular unit of instruction and observe larger numbers of learners interacting with the content, teacher capacity to see the nature of learners' intellectual tasks may deepen. Teachers may also become better able to predict learner understandings and misunderstandings. More experienced teachers may thus be better able to engage in deeper analysis of learning targets. This may be a fruitful area of inquiry regarding the development of teacher thinking and practice across early career years.

Matching and Balancing Assessments to Targets

Candidates were often surprised at the lack of balance in sets of learning targets across units—in some cases, units they had taught for years. After they completed an analysis of a unit that required the identification of the five types of learning targets, they often found they used the same type of targets repeatedly. For example, a unit may have contained three knowledge targets and one skill target but completely lacked any reasoning, product, or disposition targets. On further analysis in a revision assignment, they included a more balanced spread that then also provided options for more appropriate assessment methods.

The second assignment, related to classifying learning targets, asked candidates to match an appropriate assessment type to each learning target in a unit. In many cases, candidates found that, while the aim of a learning target was for students to gain procedural knowledge, the assessment captured only knowledge of the steps of a procedure. The same might have been true of a reasoning target that was operationalized as a knowledge target, for example aligned with a vocabulary exercise. Thus, a deeper sense of the emphasis and impact of a unit of instruction emerged as the teachers examined their existing assessment practices in light of the analysis and classification of learning targets that they had just completed.

In general, candidates experienced this portion of the course as both enlightening and enriching. Seeing the possible connections of a rich array of types of learning targets to a set of assessment options, candidates reported broadening their intentions in instructional planning beyond factual knowledge. One candidate wrote, "I always wrote learning targets, but I never thought to write targets for skills, product and disposition."

Another candidate stated:

> I am noticing that knowledge targets dominate the unit and I would like to see more reasoning targets included. Furthermore, I want to re-examine the three-dimensional (from the Next Generation Science Standards [NGSS]) target and re-work it so it is more skill or reasoning based. One of the goals of NGSS is to engage students in reasoning and argument using evidence and I would like my learning targets to reflect this.

Assessment is sometimes viewed as a discrete and technical dimension of teaching that can be addressed chiefly as a matter of learning particular skills or adopting predefined (often prepackaged and monetized) techniques. The experience of candidates engaging in this program suggests that, as an integral part of the learning process and the instructional cycle, assessment has the potential to deepen and enrich instructional goals and intentions.

Packaging Targets and Assessment at the Unit Level

Finally, the third assignment related to classifying learning targets and asked candidates to develop a unit test blueprint to ensure an appropriate and intentional mix of assessments for formative support of learning and summative evaluation.

As the next step in promoting student understanding of assessment and engagement in their own learning, candidates were encouraged to share the test blueprint with their students as yet another way of helping students understand their learning trajectory. The results illuminated the importance of including students in their own education. One middle school science teacher reported the following:

> This was a very interesting experience. . . . When I showed my students the test blueprint, they had so many questions about how education works. I learned that students thought that teachers got a giant binder from the principal that tells us exactly what to teach, similar to a massive script for the year. . . . Students complete assignments and assessments because they are told to and not because they think it will help them learn.

The act of creating the test blueprint gave many candidates a greater sense of confidence and control over their own teaching practice. It served as an opportunity for many of them to critique existing testing and assessment practices in their schools, both ones that had been developed locally and, particularly, those that were provided as part of published curricula.

Conclusion

The Creating Clear Learning Targets course supports candidates in developing a deeper understanding of how to write clear learning targets and how to help learners in the classroom understand the connection among clear learning targets, the learning activities they are asked to complete, and the assessment tasks or activities that provide evidence to guide ongoing learning.

Candidate feedback confirms that creating clear learning targets, effectively communicating the targets, and connecting the target to the activities impacts both candidate and student learning in a positive way. One kindergarten teacher stated, "This data (from a field experience assignment) showed me that students perform better when they understand what is being taught, why it is being taught, and how they will be assessed."

Modeling Student Efficacy through Candidate Efficacy

One of the foundational elements of the assessment specialization is the instructor's modeling of assessment literacy principles. The organizational structure of each course is designed to support the ongoing attainment of assessment literacy knowledge, skills, and dispositions. The topic structure adheres to a similar design for consistency but allows for freedom of choice on both how to interact with colleagues and how to complete assignments. Each topic period provides multiple opportunities for interaction. Candidates may attend a live interactive chat session, participate in several online forums, and contribute to building an assignment collaboratively.

Developing and using clear and appropriate learning targets is one of the most important steps in the instructional and classroom assessment process. Without clear learning targets, it is difficult to know how to ask questions about the state of student learning and to provide feedback to help students take the next step in their learning. This case study illustrates how a focus on developing and using clear learning targets can influence even experienced teachers' instruction.

REFLECTION QUESTIONS

1. What is the role of learning targets at different grade levels and in different content areas?
2. Are there ways of providing a direction for learning without "giving away" content that students should figure out on their own?
3. How can administrators support teachers' use of learning targets?
4. How can learning targets be used in Professional Learning Communities as teachers analyze student work?

Chapter 5

Use Purpose-Driven Assessment

Kathy S. Dyer and Jennifer Hein

SECTION BY KATHY S. DYER

What if everyone considered multiple purposes of assessment in an educational setting, including supporting student learning as well as measuring it? How might conversations, decisions, and efforts change? Assessment can be used for a variety of purposes, such as informing instructional strategies or quantifying students' knowledge at a given point in time. However, many argue that the primary focus of assessment should be to promote student learning (Black et al. 2003, 2).

Regardless of the purpose, assessments should be linked to specific educational decision-making. Who are the decision makers, and what are the decisions? Often the decision makers are considered to be the adults in the education system. However, if the group is expanded to include parents or guardians and students, a whole new world opens to each decision-making group. The decisions made by assessments can be centered on many things: program impact, student learning and differentiation, effectiveness of instructional strategies, and ensuring equity among and between individual students as well as groups of students in classrooms, schools, or across districts.

While many different types of assessment exist, this chapter will primarily discuss *formative assessment*, which is used to gather evidence of learning so that teachers can adapt instruction moment to moment, and *summative assessment*, which is designed to measure whether a student has learned specific content. To guide us, we focus on answering three questions to help us connect to the purpose of supporting student learning:

- Who will use the results?
- How will they use the results?
- What information (evidence) of student learning does the decision maker need?

Who Will Use the Results?

Decision makers in education run the gamut from policy makers to community members, but we can narrow our focus to the following groups: students, teachers, school and district leaders, and parents and community. Guess why students are listed first? Students generate the assessment information we have access to, from informal formative assessment checks during instruction to the results of an Advanced Placement (AP) exam or an ACT. They are the first users of the evidence, whether we acknowledge it or not.

Teachers make decisions minute to minute and day by day based on evidence of learning. District and school leaders need assessment results to inform decisions beyond single students and classrooms. Finally, parents and community are listed together because parents are part of the community and have an important role in informing the community about what is happening in the district and individual schools.

How Will They Use the Results?

As we consider how assessment results or evidence of learning is used, we begin to tap into the purpose-driven aspect of assessment. Students' use of assessment informs their next steps in terms of learning, motivation, and more: How hard am I going to try? Was the outcome what I thought it would be? Was the effort worth it?

From simple choices to more complex decisions (e.g., How can I do better in solving for exponents? What do I need to increase my use of evidence in my writing?), students use assessment results to inform their learning path. Becoming a self-regulated learner requires lots of information and involves many decisions.

On a daily basis, teachers make decisions regarding instruction, instructional adjustments, how to best support student learning (individually and in groups), and how to allocate their time. What needs to be communicated to whom, along with when and how that happens, is also a decision that teachers deal with regularly.

School and district leaders generate reports that are used internally and externally, by the state and community members. For accreditation purposes schools and districts aggregate and disaggregate assessment evidence so the state can make decisions about levels of success these entities demonstrate. Assessment results from both individual schools and districts may inform decisions such as what school a child attends or what yearbook a business buys an ad in.

What Information (Evidence) of Student Learning Does the Decision Maker Need?

Because each stakeholder is trying to answer different questions, the evidence of student learning needed by each varies. The idea that the purpose drives the use of an assessment is key when district and school leaders are developing a balanced approach to assessment. Students need assessment information to inform a variety of decisions, from the micro to the macro level.

Starting with the amount of effort that each student puts into the next assignment to determining which approach to comprehending a text works best for each, assessments should have a clear purpose to guide students not only in what they are learning but also in how they are learning to allow them to plan for their next steps in their learning path.

The definition of formative assessment from the Council of Chief State School Officers (2018, 2) clearly outlines the purpose for this type of assessment as designed to allow students and teachers "to elicit and use evidence of student learning to improve student understanding of intended disciplinary learning outcomes and support students to become self-directed learners."

While teachers' purposes for using assessment results may vary between "instructional management (e.g., categorizing students according to achievement levels)" and "instructional improvement (e.g., diagnosing student mistakes)" (Datnow and Hubbard 2015, 12), it is important that teachers have (1) a purpose in mind when administering an assessment and (2) definite plans in place to use the results. Once teachers have gathered evidence and interpreted it, they must translate that interpretation into pedagogical moves.

Helping school and district leaders see assessment purposes beyond state accountability, beyond funding and programmatic decisions, is critical. All those decisions chart the course of schools and districts and miss an essential element of purpose-driven assessment—the idea that assessment can further and support learning (Bonner 2013, 97). Next, Jennifer Hein illustrates how district and school leaders can foster a balanced assessment culture that supports teaching in building purposeful formative assessment practices that remain student-centered.

CASE STUDY BY JENNIFER HEIN

Reflections from the Field

In the United States, conversations about assessment and education are all too often centered on mandated or accountability-based assessments and the high-stakes data from those assessments. Decision makers and educators need other ways of measuring student learning and growth and instructional impact. There must be a greater balance between using accountability-driven assessments and using astutely developed assessments of student learning, ability, and growth. Educators and leaders must be able to use assessment data to make timely decisions, meet students where they are, and push all students to higher and deeper levels of learning and doing.

Assessment is all too often considered to be complicated and burdensome. But it does not have to be. Assessment is simply the process of gaining insight into what students know and are able to do. Some assessments are formal (e.g., quiz, project, rubric), while others are informal (e.g., exit slips, thumbs up or thumbs down, strategic questioning). Some are formative (used to inform learning) and some are summative (used to take a look back at what was learned). Regardless of the type, the knowledge gleaned about students from assessment should be thoughtfully communicated and strategically used to inform instructional decisions.

Many parents, educators, and teacher advocacy groups are skeptical that state-mandated accountability assessments improve student achievement or ensure effective instruction. Parents and teachers alike generally want to know things about student learning not always revealed by high-stakes assessments. Parents want to know if their child is on track with peers, what their child's strengths and weaknesses are, and what they can do to provide support. Teachers want to know if students have met learning targets, how to differentiate for students who need greater challenge or more support, and when to make instructional changes. This type of information is found at the classroom level, through teacher-generated assessments of student ability and learning.

Assessments with Purpose

Regardless of the nature of the assessment, assessments are more informative when they are purposeful and their data is used in intentional and authentic ways. Assessments are purposeful when they are useful to the people taking the assessment, as well as to the people using the data from the assessment.

The National Task Force on Assessment Education (2016) outlines that purpose can be determined by answering three questions:

- Who will use the results?
- What will they use them to accomplish?
- And, therefore, what information about student learning does the user need?

These questions provide an opportunity to reflect on the intended assessment and data audience, the need for and use of assessment data, and the intended measures gleaned from the assessment.

When thinking about purposeful assessment, there are four primary considerations. The first consideration is that the assessment should be designed to measure student growth, learning, or ability. Purposeful assessments are always directly aligned to instruction and assess the intended outcome of a lesson, standard, or unit.

The second consideration of purposeful assessment is that there must be understanding about what the assessment data mean or an understanding of the information the assessment provides. The third consideration is that there must be authentic, timely communication (with those being assessed, with other stakeholders, or with both) regarding what the assessment data mean or indicate. The fourth consideration associated with purposeful assessment is that the data from the assessment is used to make decisions about students or instruction.

Promoting Equity

In talking about purposeful assessment, the focus is on all students. Assessment designed and administered thoughtfully provides opportunity for equity. Paying attention to bias in all phases of the assessment process supports this opportunity—when developing or selecting, administering, scoring or grading, and even reporting results (Bonner 2013, 100; Joint Committee on Standards for Educational Evaluation 2015, 5). That means educators pay attention to the method of assessment as well as the content of assessment.

Purpose-driven assessment, or assessment and measurement that has meaning or relevance, is central to having reliable data (Bonner 2013, 87). When assessments are purpose driven, the data connected to those assessments are rich and can support impactful decision-making. Often when assessment is based on compliance alone and the purpose is not understood, the assessment and any connected data lose meaning for those taking the assessment, those measured by the assessment, and those trying to make decisions based on the assessment data.

Fostering a Positive Culture

Given the role and importance of assessment and data use in education, what must school leaders do to create a balanced, positive culture centered on assessment literacy? How can principals support teachers in creating and using formative, purpose-driven assessments?

- School leaders (i.e., school boards, central office leaders, and building-level leaders) must create and nurture a balanced, data-informed culture focused on assessment literacy.
- School leaders must provide professional development and learning opportunities about how to design and operationalize purposeful assessments, understand and use assessment data, and communicate assessment results to students and parents.
- School leaders must encourage teacher leaders and assessment superstars to share best practices and utilize them to coach others.
- School leaders must have open conversations about data use and assessment expectations.
- School leaders must act as instructional leaders, use data transparently, and be data literate decision makers.

As a high school principal and state leadership coach, Dr. Hein understood the importance of understanding data and was accustomed to making data-informed leadership decisions. However, when she moved from a large urban city in Tennessee to Western North Carolina to serve as the principal of a rural high school, what she did not know was the local district and school context.

So, during the application process, she spent considerable time developing an understanding of student assessment in North Carolina and analyzing district- and school-level state data. Once hired, she began to dig into the school's historical data, as well as student assessment data, to identify strengths, areas for growth, and trends.

She spent time over the summer learning about the needs of the school community and the assessment and data culture of both the district and school. Her first few days as the new principal included meeting with teacher leaders and other administrators to make programmatic, master scheduling, and student placement decisions.

During the summer she held strengths, weaknesses, opportunities, and threats (SWOT) analysis meetings with students, parents, community members, teachers, and central office personnel to learn the strengths and areas for growth of the faculty. In those meetings, she learned that teachers cared deeply about students and were committed to the school. She also learned the strengths and areas for improvement among teachers. Specifically, she discerned that many teachers needed support in understanding the school's formal, summative assessment data and how to effectively create and use purposeful assessments (e.g., differentiation, pacing, instructional strategies) to measure student learning and make instructional decisions.

Dr. Hein knew that understanding the district and school context was just one part of creating a culture of assessment literacy and that, if the school was going to have a balanced, positive culture of assessment and data use, the discussion had to ultimately center on teacher-designed, formative, purposeful assessment practices.

After school opened, she began having departmental meetings, reviewing teacher lesson plans, and conducting classroom walkthroughs to get a sense of teachers' instructional styles, classroom environments, teacher strengths, classroom resource needs, and future professional development focus areas. After several months, she then worked with other building administrators and teacher leaders to develop a yearlong plan to support teachers and increase student learning opportunities to ensure equity in educational opportunity. The plan focused on the following elements:

- creating a balanced, positive culture of assessment literacy;
- designing targeted professional development and teacher learning opportunities centered on purposeful, formative classroom assessment;
- using effective, superstar teachers to share assessment practices;
- having transparent conversations with stakeholders, students, and teachers about school data; the use of formative, teacher-designed assessment; and the use of data to make student-centered decisions;
- creating clear expectations for using assessments to support student learning and effective instruction;
- ensuring student-centered and data-informed administrative team decisions.

Empowering Educators

The first step, creating a culture of assessment literacy, meant working with students, teachers, parents, and community members to understand that a central purpose of assessment and data collection is to support effective instruction and student learning. There was a need to foster conversation about how summative assessments (e.g., school report cards, grades, end-of-course tests, ACT, Advanced Placement, and final exams) were used to measure student learning and how teachers' use of formative assessment supporte students.

With teachers, initial conversations were focused on defining assessment in terms other than summative, formal, and state- and district-mandated assessments. Teachers met with Dr. Hein in subject-specific focus groups to discuss everyday ways student learning was being measured in the classroom and how those assessments were being used.

Dr. Hein conducted classroom walkthrough observations and asked students directly, "What are you supposed to know and be able to do as a result of your time in class today?" Some students knew, through their teacher's use of purposeful, clear targets or student learning outcome statements, while others did not know. She noted student motivation and achievement in classrooms where teachers used learning statements and openly communicated learning goals with students to determine trends and patterns and to have conversations with teachers about their instruction and students.

Initial professional development sessions were designed to be targeted and supportive and to create a balanced, positive assessment culture. They were also meant to give teachers learning opportunities centered on purposeful, formative classroom assessment.

In the first few sessions, teachers were asked to create student-friendly learning targets or goal statements based on curriculum standards. Teachers worked collaboratively, by subject area, to determine appropriate learning levels (e.g., understand, judge, create) using Bloom's taxonomy (1956, 20) and the work of Robert Marzano (2001, 1–25). Teachers then designed evaluations or assessments of the learning in connection to the learning level target. From that point, teachers were asked to backward-design a lesson or unit so that the learning target, instruction or activity, and assessment were aligned.

Teachers who were efficient in using clear targets and creating aligned assessments were asked to share best practices with the faculty in Superstar Assessment infomercials. Teachers highlighted in these infomercials were celebrated as Superstar Assessment Leaders. Dr. Hein, assistant principals, and those teacher leaders then met to set school-level goals for full implementation of the use of clear targets.

Dr. Hein and the administrative team continued to engage in classroom walkthroughs looking for the effective use and communication of student learning outcome statements. Teachers were encouraged to be creative with posting their targets, and they had the opportunity to observe other teachers to learn how they used targets in their classrooms. Teachers who needed extra support received coaching along the way from Superstar Assessment Leaders and administrators.

Subsequent professional development sessions centered on having teachers think about daily, informal, formative measurement or assessment of student learning in relation to the intended target. Faculty were asked to think about ways to illicit, from students, their interpretation of their learning in connection with the learning target. This step was important to encourage students to think and talk about their own learning and for teachers to make instructional shifts when students were not on target.

After a few months of practice using and discussing learning targets, Dr. Hein did more classroom walkthroughs to look for learning targets and discuss with students what they were learning. Over those few months, students had not only grown accustomed to looking for learning targets to guide their knowledge of what they were supposed to know and be able to do, but they had come to expect them. During these walkthroughs, when Dr. Hein asked what students were learning, they were able to explain the activity and target, as well as assess their learning.

Collective Support

The School Improvement Team (SIT), a team of twenty-five to thirty parents, teachers, and community members, helped shift the assessment culture of the school. These regularly scheduled meetings were purposefully free of education speak. Initial meetings provided a platform for parents and community members to share what they wanted to know about how students were progressing and what they were learning.

Subsequent conversations centered on the reasons and best practices for formative assessment, the new professional development teachers were receiving, and the rollout of a schoolwide use of clear learning targets. Throughout the school year, Dr. Hein, teachers, and students shared successes and taught stakeholders how to ask students about what they were learning and if they accomplished their learning goals.

After several months of professional development learning opportunities, conversations, coaching sessions, and classroom walkthroughs, the school began to look very different. While some teachers still struggled with designing student learning outcomes, communicating with individual students about what the assessment data meant, or using formative assessment to make instructional decisions, the majority were effective at this type of purposeful, formative assessment. Again, teachers who needed more coaching were coached and supported.

After another few months, when conducting classroom walkthroughs, students, often without being asked, would share with administrators the clear learning targets and could have conversations about where they were succeeding and where they were struggling. Parents and guardians began to communicate with teachers and school leaders how much they appreciated the new and robust conversations about their student's educational experiences and thoughts about their own learning.

This focused professional development paid off. Students appreciated being informed about what they were supposed to be able to know and do. As teachers began to perfect the use of learning targets, design purposeful assessments aligned to lessons and targets, and use assessment results, rather than solely grades, they were better able to understand student learning.

When teachers began to gather student feedback on attainment of the learning target and use that feedback to adjust pacing, differentiate instruction, and shift strategies, they felt empowered. The intentional use of learning targets to help students focus on their own learning outcomes and to provide teachers with timely, incremental, formative measures of student learning shifted the culture of assessment and balanced the use of data in Dr. Hein's school.

Part of the balanced culture of assessment was tied to impactful instructional leadership. Dr. Hein and her administrative team provided clear expectations for the use of formative assessment and held frequent assessment check-ins with teachers to ensure they and their students were seeing the benefits of purposeful, formative assessments. In addition, Dr. Hein, the administrative team, and the leadership team were transparent about how they used data to make student-centered and data-informed decisions in areas such as course design, course scheduling, teacher course assignment, and school assessment practices.

An example of a course-design decision included extending Algebra I from one semester to two for students who had not reached math grade-level proficiency in sixth, seventh, or eighth grade and did not obtain a specific score on a teacher-created, collaboratively designed assessment of math knowledge necessary to ensure success.

Student attendance and teacher-issued grade data helped inform decisions about when certain classes would be offered. Examples included not offering senior English in the spring term during the first or last period of the day and ensuring math and science courses were not split by lunch. Assigning courses moved beyond teacher requests to making these decisions using multiple teacher data points and previous student data points.

Ensuring equity in educational opportunity, supporting student learning, and making impactful decisions about students, instruction, and programs requires that assessment audiences (e.g., school districts, policy makers, governments, principals, teachers, parents, students) use reliable data and have a keen understanding of what the data mean. One component of assessment is understanding that reliability is directly connected to purpose.

While teachers and leaders will likely use state and district summative assessment data in the foreseeable future, they must also focus on informal, purposeful assessments of student learning. In sum, district and school leaders must foster a balanced assessment culture and support teachers in developing purposeful formative assessment practices aligned to intended outcomes, encourage them to authentically communicate with students and other stakeholders what students know and are able to do, and ensure they make data-informed instructional and student-centered decisions.

REFLECTION QUESTIONS

1. How might school leaders foster a balanced assessment culture? How do they know when the balance is reached?
2. How is assessment design, and use, connected to ensuring equity in educational opportunity? When might assessment design and data use not promote equity, and what can educators do about it?
3. If school stakeholders must be assessment and data literate to make effective decisions that promote equity, how do they become assessment literate? What trainings do parents, school board members, and community members receive?

Chapter 6

Joining Forces with Colleagues[1]

Amelia Wenk Gotwals, Denny Chandler, Melissa Spadin, and Heather Lageman

SECTION BY AMELIA WENK GOTWALS

It is possible for teachers to go through the school day with their doors closed and not have job-related conversations with colleagues. In fact, teaching can often be a very private occupation. While it is sometimes nice to shut the door and have time with just students, having opportunities to work with colleagues can produce fruitful outcomes.

In fact, often the best learning experiences involve working with colleagues. By sharing teaching successes and struggles, teachers can take advantage of colleagues' knowledge and experience (Wilson and Berne 1999, 195). This chapter describes the research base behind the importance of joining forces with colleagues to support learning about assessment. In addition, it presents two case studies about statewide programs designed to support assessment literacy.

Having opportunities to join forces with colleagues is important because learning is a social process. One of the most widely used collaborative professional learning opportunities in schools is professional learning communities or PLCs (e.g., Grossman, Wineburg, and Woolworth 2001, 943). As all teachers know, there is a big difference between a group of educators getting together to talk and an effective PLC. While having time to talk is important and enjoyable, effective PLCs support teachers in thinking deeply about their instruction and can lead to changes in practice.

Characteristics of Effective Professional Learning Communities

Effective PLCs have several common characteristics, including that they are not "one-shot deals." Rather, effective PLCs often last for months or years because learning and changing classroom practices take time (Wei, Darling-Hammond, and Adamson 2010, 57).

Another characteristic of effective PLCs is that members have developed a supportive community with shared norms and values (Newmann, King, and Youngs 2000; Stoll et al. 2006; Wenger 1998). Sometimes discussion in PLCs can remain surface level, with teachers sharing ideas and colleagues offering praise (Kintz et al. 2015, 130). However, for PLCs to be effective, discussion should allow for colleagues to provide constructive criticism. In fact, Wilson and Berne (1999, 195) suggest that productive PLCs must focus on building "trust and community while aiming for a professional discourse that includes and does not avoid critique."

Building the trust necessary to have these types of deeper conversations in PLCs can be difficult for both the person sharing ideas and the people responding. It can be hard to share ideas and data that may expose struggles teachers are having. In addition, educators may find it challenging to provide constructive criticism in a way that helps their colleagues without making them defensive (Lord 1994, 192). However, having shared norms and values can make sharing ideas, successes, and struggles more comfortable.

Norms can be achieved through the use of protocols that provide guidelines for having productive conversations. These protocols can provide clear opportunities to present problems for which teachers want help as well as ways of providing critique that is supportive of colleagues' efforts (Horn and Little 2009, 211; Nelson et al. 2008, 1274). Using protocols based on shared norms and values can clarify expectations about how colleagues will work together to achieve their goals.

Another common characteristic of effective PLCs is that there is a shared vision for the purpose and direction of the collaboration (Penuel et al. 2007, 944). This purpose should be aligned with district, school, and teacher goals for student outcomes (Newmann, King, and Youngs 2000, 267). When PLCs have a clear focus on improving instruction and student learning, the purpose for discussions can be targeted (Wayne et al. 2008, 473). Just as learning targets can align instruction and assessment for students and teachers in classrooms, as discussed in chapter 4, having a shared vision can align the work of PLCs.

Having a common understanding of the purpose for working together can also make sharing aspects of teaching practice more comfortable. When all members are working together toward a common goal, the types of supportive yet constructively critical collaborations are more common (Kintz et al. 2015, 132).

A final common characteristic of effective PLCs is that they offer opportunities to make clear connections between student outcomes and "concrete tasks of teaching, assessment, observation and reflection" (Wei, Darling-Hammond, and McLaughlin 1995, 598). Easton (2008, 756) argues that the most powerful learning opportunities are closely tied to teachers' work. In PLCs, this type of work may involve participation in a "cycle of inquiry" in which teachers can "go through recursive stages of formulating problems, collecting data, analyzing data, reporting results, and planning for action" (Levine 2010, 112). This type of process promotes teacher learning, which can lead to changes in teachers' practice (Webster-Wright 2009, 713).

Collaborative Learning about Assessment

All of the characteristics of effective PLCs discussed earlier hold true in the case of supporting assessment literacy in education systems (e.g., Popham 2009, 9; Schneider and Randel 2009, 261). For example, PLCs can offer a designated space for meaningful discussion about assessment and other student learning data. When teachers use common assessments, they can compare results and share promising instructional approaches that foster student learning in PLCs.

PLCs can also support teachers in discussing their formative assessment practices (Black and Wiliam 2005; Shepard 2000; Webb and Jones 2009).

> Formative assessment is a planned, ongoing process used by all students and teachers during learning and teaching to elicit and use evidence of student learning to improve student understanding of intended disciplinary learning outcomes and support students to become more self-directed learners. (Formative Assessment for Students and Teachers 2017, 1–2).

By focusing on clear formative assessment strategies and tools, teachers can learn from each other and make changes in their formative assessment practices (Sato 2003, 115). This chapter highlights two case studies that discuss how state-level programs can be used to support assessment literacy.

In the first case study, Denny Chandler recounts how a school administrator supported his district in using the Formative Assessment for Michigan Educators (FAME) program to promote student learning. In the second case study, Melissa Spadin and Heather Lageman describe their journey to advocate for assessment literacy across Maryland.

CASE STUDY BY DENNY CHANDLER

The Hesperia Story: The Focus Is on the Students

School administrators face a number of different and often conflicting challenges. On the one hand, they must be managers of budgets and supervisors of personnel. These responsibilities often make it difficult for an administrator to be an instructional leader and a catalyst for change. On the other hand, principals are responsible for providing instructional leadership and improving teaching and learning in their buildings. This case study shares the story of how one school administrator became involved with the FAME (Formative Assessment for Michigan Educators) program and, through his involvement, worked to support teacher learning about formative assessment.

About FAME

FAME is a joint effort of the Michigan Department of Education (MDE) and the Michigan Assessment Consortium (MAC). The overarching goal of the FAME program is to help educators learn about and use the formative assessment process in classroom instruction. MDE conducts FAME workshops and provides other services for educators to help them develop school-based "Learning Teams."

The program provides resources on formative assessment research, theory, and practice to promote teachers' capacity to reflect on, implement, and refine their instructional and assessment practices in the classroom. To achieve these goals, FAME provides support to Learning Teams in which a group of educators and a Coach work collaboratively to learn about and practice the formative assessment process in local contexts.

Since its inception in 2008, FAME has worked to address MDE's goal of providing different approaches to reach high school students who are low achievers. Initially, MDE partnered with Measured Progress to develop and implement the FAME program. After several years, MAC took the place of Measured Progress. According to Kim Young, who directs FAME for MDE,

"The formative assessment process is an essential part of a comprehensive assessment system. By financially supporting and endorsing FAME, the MDE is sending a strong message of the importance of formative assessment." See Table 6.1 for an outline of the FAME formative assessment components.

Table 6.1 FAME Components and Elements

Guiding Questions	FAME Components and Elements
Where are we (teacher and students) going?	**Planning** 1.1—Instructional Planning: planning based on knowledge of the content, standards, pedagogy, formative assessment process, and students. **Learning Target Use** 2.1—Designing Learning Targets: the use and communication of daily instructional aims with the students 2.2—Learning Progressions: connection of the learning target to past and future learning 2.3—Models of Proficient Achievement: examples of successful work for students to use as a guide.
What does the student understand now?	**Eliciting Evidence of Student Understanding** 3.1—Activating Prior Knowledge: the opportunity for students to self-assess or connect new ideas to their prior knowledge 3.2—Gathering Evidence of Student Understanding: use of a variety of tools and strategies to gather information about student thinking and understanding regarding the learning targets from all students 3.3—Teacher Questioning Strategies: the intentional use of questions for students to explain their thinking or to connect their idea to another student's response 3.4—Skillful Use of Questions: a focus on the purpose, timing, and audience for questions to deliver content and to check students' understanding
How do we (teacher and students) get to the learning target?	**Formative Feedback** 4.1—Feedback from the Teacher: verbal or written feedback to a student to improve his or her achievement of the learning target 4.2—Feedback from Peers: feedback from one student to another student about his or her learning in relation to a learning target 4.3—Student Self-Assessment: the process in which students gather information and reflect on their own learning in relation to the learning goal. **Instructional and Learning Decisions** 5.1—Adjustments to Teaching: teachers' daily decisions about changes to instruction 5.2—Adjustments to Learning: students' use of feedback for improvement.

About the FAME Professional Learning Model

New Learning Teams form every year and engage in learning and implementing the formative assessment process. To begin the first year, new Learning Teams attend a full-day professional learning session known as "Launching into Learning," where they learn more about the FAME program and the formative assessment process. The number of new Learning Teams each year is influenced by available state and local finances and applicant location (MDE seeks to have active Learning Teams located throughout the state).

After they attend the Launch, Learning Teams begin to meet regularly to engage in collaborative inquiry about how the formative assessment process can best be enacted in team members' classrooms. Most Learning Teams meet monthly for one to three hours. Typically, Learning Teams use the resources that the FAME program provides while at the same time setting the course for learning that most benefits team members.

There are also learning opportunities for Coaches. Over time, Coaches have the opportunity to receive additional MDE-sponsored training in the Cognitive Coaching Foundation Seminar (days 1–8) and Adaptive Schools Foundation Training (days 1–4). These trainings are critical in the development of effective coaches and successful Learning Teams.

Using FAME to Support Ongoing Teacher Learning

In 2016 Vaughn White became the superintendent of Hesperia Community Schools in Hesperia, Michigan. Hesperia is a small community in West Michigan. The school district includes a high school, a middle school, and an elementary school. Serving a total student population of just over nine hundred students, the district employs about fifty faculty and support staff. The district's prominently posted mission statement is this: "The mission of Hesperia Community Schools is to provide quality educational opportunities that empower all students to become responsible, enlightened and productive citizens today and in the future." The mission's emphasis is on *students*, and this commitment requires the faculty to continually evaluate their practices and look for ways to be even more effective.

Coach White's Background

White brought twenty-eight years of experience as an educator to Hesperia, along with experience as a coach of a FAME Learning Team. White first recognized the value of FAME when he was a principal at Shelby Middle School in a different district in West Michigan. He participated in FAME training and, in his role as principal and coach, found the program to be well received by teachers and beneficial to students.

Later, White became the principal of Kingsley Middle School in Kingsley, Michigan, where he introduced FAME to a group of teachers. After the first year, the program expanded to include all middle school teachers. He combined FAME with other schoolwide initiatives, most specifically Spencer Kagan's cooperative learning structures (Kagan 1989, 12) and Robert Marzano's teacher evaluation and instructional essentials models (Marzano 2010). Dr. Kagan's work is designed to increase student motivation and engagement by the effective, structured use of cooperative learning. Dr. Marzano's research has identified ways in which teacher assessment is connected with student performance. These three initiatives (i.e., Cooperative Learning Structures, Marzano's evaluation, and FAME) supported and reinforced each other in Kingsley, where they have become part of a normal routine rather than viewed as three distinct initiatives.

When White moved to Hesperia, he saw many similarities between the two school districts, leading him to believe FAME could also be successful at Hesperia. Like in so many schools across the nation, the district faced a need to address achievement gaps between student groups. He also saw a faculty looking for direction and a meaningful approach to address this need. White's initial focus began at the middle school, where, he recognized an opportunity for the FAME initiative to be implemented.

Administrative Support in Hesperia

Hesperia benefits from a close working relationship between school principals Bryan Mey and David LaPrairie. Bryan Mey, an educator with thirteen years' experience, leads the Patricia St. Clair Elementary School, which serves students in kindergarten through fifth grade. David LaPrairie, a thirty-four-year education veteran, leads Hesperia Middle School and Hesperia High School, which serves grades six through twelve. Grade five is housed in the middle school building and is often included in the middle school structure.

When White, Mey, and LaPrairie met, much of their discussion addressed Hesperia Community Schools as a whole and not the usual differentiation that exists between elementary, middle, and high schools. Adding even more to the unity is the physical location of all three schools, which are located next to each other. Some faculty members even teach both middle and high school classes.

As with any change in leadership, White, as the new leader, had to assess the entire program and culture as it existed at Hesperia and decide where changes needed to be made. One area identified was to change instructional practice. When looking at various school initiatives, some key factors drove his decision.

White, Mey, and LaPrairie focused heavily on what research says about what works, what does not work, best practices, and what would be a good fit for Hesperia. Often the introduction of a new initiative means the end of other programs. This can lead to frustration when educators feel as if they are in a situation of continuous flux. In Hesperia, the leaders wanted an initiative that would fit and support the good work already taking place. They wanted to avoid adding another layer of work and instead design an initiative that would become part of the existing fabric of professional development, positively impacting teacher instruction and student achievement.

Based on his prior experiences, White felt FAME would be an excellent fit. FAME's research base and its emphasis on allowing teachers to learn about the formative assessment process and engaging students as responsible participants in their learning were important factors in his decision.

"FAME itself sets up the structure," White said. "You have the kick-off to get everybody on board. You set up your teams, and you develop your leadership. You have the Adaptive School and Cognitive Coaching to support the leadership and it propels you through.... It's an inclusive learning process."

District Approach

The first year, the administrators decided to take small steps by establishing only one Learning Team. Over time, FAME researchers have found that many schools and districts start modestly. They form one learning team and use it as a gauge to measure how it might be received throughout the school or district. What often happens is that the local FAME participants, the students, and FAME program leaders encourage others to be involved. This is the approach that was used in Kingsley, and it would be the approach used in Hesperia.

The first FAME Learning Team at Hesperia included the two principals, three middle school classroom teachers and one high school classroom teacher. Teachers Deb Claeys, Audrey Fosburg, Melissa Baker, and Justin Zeerip brought to the team many years of education experience; by the 2018–2019 school year, they were three-year veterans of FAME.

How It Worked

One important feature of FAME is the training provided by the MDE. White and his team attended a FAME Launching into Learning session, which annually offers Learning Teams the opportunity to collaborate and share with each other. The Coach is part of the Learning Team, and all are considered "students" who are learning about the formative assessment process together.

At a Launch, educators are encouraged to share their ideas and experiences with each other. The desire is to create an environment of trust so that participants will become comfortable sharing their thoughts and practices with other members of the team. They are also encouraged to offer and receive feedback, for it is only through reflection and discussion that teachers can make meaningful changes in their classrooms. This process is to be continued through the rest of the school year during Learning Team meetings.

For many first-year teams, most work focuses on becoming familiar with the FAME Components and Elements. They form the foundation of the program, introducing formative assessment as a process with five distinct components: (1) planning, (2) learning target use, (3) eliciting evidence of student understanding, (4) formative feedback, and (5) instructional and learning decisions. Each Component has associated "Elements" or practices. For many, this process can be somewhat overwhelming; however, the FAME Learning Team, as facilitated by the Coach, determines how they will proceed.

At the Launch, many Learning Team members come to realize they have some familiarity with the Components or Elements. The major difference, however, is understanding how the Components and Elements work together and support each other, creating the formative assessment process. Participants also realize that, while they may refer to some of the Components or Elements, they are not taking a preplanned and intentional approach. By establishing a base of understanding and exploring each Component and Element, teachers are able to incorporate the process so that it becomes a seamless and integrated part of their instruction and student learning. They truly adopt the formative assessment process.

Decisions about which initiatives and programs to incorporate in Hesperia are made by the administrators with input from teachers. As previously noted, looking at the research and data is a crucial first step. They also consider how new elements fit into their school and faculty and with other ongoing initiatives.

"Staff buy-in is important," David LaPrairie said. "So much of having staff buy-in is how you do it, how you roll or lay things out. We take strategic steps, not just to go slow, but to do them in step with instructional staff. We're sharing with them . . . so we ask, 'How is it going? Do you feel this would be a good thing to take on?' There have been green lights on all."

It was imperative that the first year of FAME implementation be a success and that success become the driving force to expand to the rest of the middle school. While sustaining and expanding FAME was key, the most critical consideration was the impact of using the formative assessment process in participants' classrooms. Teachers needed to believe their hard work and study had the intended outcomes.

At the conclusion of the first year of study and practice, the administrators decided to expand FAME at the middle school. The first-year Learning Team members became the Coaches who co-facilitated the new Learning Teams. This additional level of support for Coaches helped them share the load of facilitation as they continued to learn about formative assessment with their new Learning Teams.

Progress Status

Based on the experiences in years one and two, participants added two new Learning Teams and Coaches, for a total of five teams in the program's third year. By the start of the 2018–19 school year, almost every middle school and high school teacher participated in a FAME Learning Team, each proceeding at its own pace. As the FAME Coaches reflect on their Coaching experiences, they report slow and steady progress. They describe two different audiences when they look at their work in FAME to date.

The first audience is the other teachers who make up their Learning Teams. The goal for Learning Team meetings is for participants to learn about the different Components—from the FAME resources and from their own experiences. As noted earlier, one advantage is that many of the teachers already use some of the Components and Elements being studied. They do, however, come to realize they need to be more purposeful and intentional in how they plan, incorporate, and use the information provided by the students.

The second primary audience is the students. As with teachers, students are familiar with certain parts of the formative assessment process; however, more work is needed in other areas. Students readily understand the importance of knowing the learning targets, but they often struggle with self-assessment. They find it difficult to self-assess in a way that provides direction on how to improve. The more teachers become comfortable in using the formative assessment process, the more students will see the benefits.

Deb, Justin, Audrey, and Melissa, the original Learning Team members and now Coaches—along with their Learning Teams—are able to focus even more on classroom practice. New Coaches and Learning Teams work on establishing a foundation of learning about the formative assessment process. Vincent Grodus, one of the new Coaches, believes that he and his Team will need to "lean on" the existing teams for support and guidance. This is an ongoing process, as Hesperia supports the multiyear FAME commitment and the continuing support of other district initiatives on the way to making meaningful change.

"This is a perpetual cycle of best practices," Bryan Mey said. "Schools that do those handful of things really, really well, and they continue to do them year after year, those are the schools that really move the needle."

Future Plans

White, Mey, and LaPrairie continue to provide support as instructional leaders, but they also want to give the Learning Teams space. The continuation of FAME is not their decision alone. Rather, it will be based on how Learning Teams determine the extent of their own learning, how it affects classroom instruction, and the impact it has on students. The leaders know this commitment takes time and hard work. They also know it gives their students the opportunity to succeed.

White was asked by a teacher, "When do I know I'm at the top of my teaching career?" His response: "You will know you're at the top when you look at each student in your classroom and you know, before they take the summative assessment, how they are going to score."

As shared at the beginning, the mission statement of Hesperia Community Schools is to provide students an education that prepares them for the future. It is this combination of instructional leadership, dedicated teachers, and engaged students that will allow Hesperia to achieve this mission. FAME and the formative assessment process are an integral part of this commitment.

Related Links

The following video segments help illustrate selected FAME experiences in Hesperia:

- Hesperia Administrators Talk about FAME, https://vimeo.com/310174069/0cd0ca6fe0
- Hesperia Administrators: FAME and Other Initiatives, https://vimeo.com/290740007/8463aaa8c6
- Hesperia Coaches Reflect Back, https://vimeo.com/290743163/08a84ad0e8
- Hesperia Coaches Share Expectations, https://vimeo.com/290744243/4095aed981

CASE STUDY BY MELISSA SPADIN AND HEATHER LAGEMAN

Maryland's Journey toward Assessment Literacy

The most difficult part of having a deep enduring passion for assessment literacy is accepting that not everyone feels the same way. Assessment belongs to everybody and nobody—while it is an integral part of teaching and learning, accountability measures, and even access to college or career programs, it is often seen as an "other" or additional layer that is not always held up with the same importance.

Maryland has been working on building assessment literacy since 2013 through both convergent and divergent avenues. The key lesson learned along the way is that assessment literacy cannot be developed alone; instead, advocates must leverage connections and pool resources to increase their reach.

Central to this outreach in Maryland was starting small with a refined message and staying true to the central idea, while also being flexible to meet the needs of specific groups. Importantly, within that flexibility is a need to create and use language that is free of assumptions about where educators are on their path toward assessment literacy. Just as teachers are expected to do in the classroom, it is critical to personalize the message about assessment literacy to any audience for whatever entry point they have.

This case study describes the journey of advocacy. It considers how the work was initiated, how the message was crafted, how collegial collaboration was solicited and organized, and how customized language was used to appeal to the aims and needs of the particular stakeholder with the goals of transfer, spread, and ultimately sustainability. In Maryland, the collaboration began in 2013 due to a convergence of Race to the Top (RTTT) projects, including the Educator Effectiveness Academies/Maryland College and Career Ready Conferences project, and the Formative Assessment for Maryland Educators (FAME) project. Below these projects are described.

Educator Effectiveness Academies/Maryland College and Career Ready Conferences Project

The goal of the initial Academies and Conferences project was designing learning opportunities for teachers to sustain their implementation of new college- and career-ready standards. The focus of the first set of learning opportunities was providing effective support for teachers and administrators in every public school in Maryland to effectively implement all aspects of Maryland's reform plan associated with the new standards.

These learning opportunities specifically supported the work of transitioning to new curriculum and assessments in every district. Educator Effectiveness Academies provided high-quality professional development for administrators and tenured teachers in teams (one coach or teacher leader in each content area of reading/English language arts, mathematics and STEM [Science, Technology, Engineering and Mathematics]) from each of the 1,400 schools in Maryland. Administrators received similar but differentiated training as appropriate. This was a three-year investment (five days of training in the summer and two days during the school year for each of three years from 2011 to 2013) to ensure that the school teams had the skills and materials to support teachers in their schools.

Content in the Academies focused on the following:

- effective strategies for implementing curriculum based on the Common Core State Standards;
- using the new formative, interim, and summative assessments;
- using the Instructional Improvement System (IIS) and Online Instructional Toolkits.

Master teachers were recruited and contracted to deliver instruction each year in the face-to-face Academies in seven regions throughout the state.

After three years of the Educator Effectiveness Academies, the Maryland College and Career Ready Conferences offered a personalized professional learning experience for 3,700 volunteer Maryland educators. The conferences offered over 140 different topical sessions on the new learning standards, allowing attendees to participate in the sessions that best met their needs and the needs of their schools. The content of the sessions was determined through feedback gathered from site visits that the Maryland State Department of Education (MSDE) curriculum and assessment staff conducted in every local school system in the state during the 2013–14 school year.

Throughout the evolution of this process, the professional learning team looked at the intersection of teacher development and the observation and evaluation process. Members of the team focused on how to effect teaching best practices that improve student achievement. It was essential to focus on how anchor standards build disciplinary bridges and create a common thread so that everyone can speak the same language, build disciplinary literacy, and collaborate through a core understanding.

Formative Assessment for Maryland Educators (FAME) Project

One instructional practice that the professional team determined was worthy of focus was formative assessment. Thus, the Formative Assessment for Maryland Educators (FAME) project was started. The FAME project progressed in fits and starts. Some of the struggles were because the members had to build an audience and demonstrate a need for work on formative assessment to occur in schools and districts. The team acknowledged that while wide-spread partnerships were the goal, it was first necessary to build partnerships through existing relationships.

Thus, the team began a campaign of winning hearts and minds. The members focused on a shared vision for high-quality teaching and learning (hearts) and the research base/funding that accompanied the project (minds). Each team member was assigned to build relationships with others in the education world outside of the team. By focusing on building relationships, the FAME team members were able to learn about the current needs and issues of various stakeholders. They were then able to discuss how formative assessment might be part of a solution to meet these stakeholders' needs.

While the team was building these relationships, the MSDE was also working on transitioning the state assessment system to Partnership for Assessment of Readiness for College and Careers (PARCC). Part of PARCC included the design and implementation of a formative assessment system, including a formative assessment item bank with items aligned to the new standards.

In spring 2014, the MSDE piloted five online professional development modules as part of its FAME initiative. In addition to the modules, the FAME program also included classroom application activities and building-level focus groups designed to support formative assessment implementation in schools.

In summer 2014, the MSDE conducted leadership training for principals, facilitators, and central office staff participating in FAME during the 2014–15 school year. The state also conducted summer leadership institutes for educators from thirty-six schools in twelve districts focused on utilizing formative assessments in the classroom. The result of these partnerships was collaboration with and learning from colleagues as well as the opportunity to present at network meetings, which ultimately led to wider participation across the state.

When FAME participants were surveyed, results revealed that very few had learned about the cohort as a requirement from leadership. Instead, most participants had heard about FAME from the school level or from the content specialists who saw the need for greater understanding of formative assessment in their field. During the first year of FAME implementation, care was taken to include MSDE content coordinators as well as district-level leaders in leadership training, community-of-practice meetings, and additional supporting events such as webinars, conference presentations, and the midyear FAME "Road Trip."

The professional learning team was a partner in all of this work, from designing and supporting webinars to attending events and community-of-practice meetings. This collaborative work, in conjunction with advocacy from the director of curriculum, led to a wider conversation about the supports necessary to create the systems change they were working toward.

While the initial focus was formative assessment and supporting the implementation of new state standards, conversations began about what could help change instructional practice on a larger scale. It became clear that the unifier was a need for assessment literacy for all stakeholders in the education system, from classroom teachers to legislators, and everyone in between. This realization led to a new project named the Maryland Assessment Literacy Collaborative (MALC).

Shifting the Focus to Assessment Literacy

The first step for MALC was to articulate a clear vision: "The purpose of the MALC is to develop the assessment literacy of all Maryland educators to improve student learning with regionally based support and professional learning." The design of MALC was intended to increase regional collaboration and participation. The group accomplished this goal by holding regional meetings that served as both learning and sharing opportunities.

Ultimately, the hope (and outcome) was that a wider collection of stakeholders would attend. The MALC convenings were also useful for those leading the sessions. For example, MSDE staff could quickly evaluate knowledge, misconceptions, and gaps in understanding about assessment and design future meetings and technical support to meet identified needs.

The work with MALC lead to several opportunities reaching additional stakeholders as well. Staff were invited to lead learning with the Maryland Association of Boards of Education (MABE), develop data literacy workshops held throughout the state, and advise the Commission to Review Maryland's Use of Assessments in Public Schools.

In the background of these collaborative events were many ongoing partnerships working to build and strengthen assessment literacy. These partnerships provided important opportunities to gain insight into practices in other states, share and develop resources, and create alliances to move the work forward.

For example, the Council of Chief State Schools Officers (CCSSO) holds meetings about assessment through its State Collaborative on Assessment and Student Standards (SCASS) workgroups. The FAME team attended the Formative Assessment for Students and Teachers (FAST) SCASS. This partnership gave the team exposure to assessment literacy resources and learning developed in other states, as well as insight into the policy and implementation moves necessary for a successful rollout.

As part of FAST SCASS, Maryland had the opportunity to learn from the high-quality assessment literacy online modules offered by the Colorado Department of Education and review the newest version of FAME out of

Oregon, called the Oregon Formative Assessment for Students and Teachers (OFAST). The Maryland team was also able to develop professional learning, conference presentations, and gain insight into best practice from around the world.

The Continued Influence of FAME

While neither of the authors currently work with the MSDE, they have continued their collaboration and commitment to promoting assessment literacy through collaborative methods.

Spadin moved to the San Diego County Office of Education as a coordinator of assessment, accountability, and evaluation, while Lageman returned to her previous district, Baltimore County Public Schools, as the executive director of leadership development. Their new positions came with different demands, but also a new group of colleagues to learn from and with. While the structure, laws, processes, and accountability system were significantly different in California, Spadin found that the need for assessment literacy remained the same.

Spadin's first step in gaining the trust and building relationships with her new colleagues was to learn the history of assessment in California and how it played out in each of the content areas, as well as current initiatives in each area.

The California Department of Education has published frameworks to accompany the standards in each content area to provide guidance on implementation of the standards. Each framework contains a chapter dedicated entirely to assessment of the content. However, through conversations with teachers and administrators, it became clear that the majority of their work was focused on the teaching and learning side of implementing the standards, with less focus given to assessment. This was not because of a lack of interest, but instead a lack of time, capacity, and support needed to advance disciplinary assessment literacy.

Spadin's next step was one of the key lessons: start small, with a coalition of the willing. She began sharing some of her previous work—in formative assessment, assessment literacy, and task design—to determine both current interest and comfort levels. Spadin also began attending professional learning offerings and content area meetings to understand current areas of focus and how assessment work could be integrated into existing systems and processes.

A common thread quickly emerged in the need for a focus on developing and implementing performance assessments to be used as formative, curriculum-embedded tasks as well as summative tools to certify learning.

In fall 2018, Spadin began focused collaborations with specific content areas to develop introductory and in-depth professional learning about assessment in the area. She established monthly meetings covering performance assessment, using an inquiry model to learn collaboratively. This collaboration has produced co-led or co-developed presentations in nearly all content areas, work plans that include explicit collaborative events or products for the 2019–20 school year, and district-elicited projects for assessment in the content areas.

Since Spadin's arrival, her colleagues have reported an increase in both knowledge about assessment and comfort with discussing assessment in their work. English language arts (ELA) Coordinator Cherissa Beck, a consistent collaborator, explains the need for deeper learning about assessment:

> We teach unique individuals, and each unique, individual student deserves to have instruction that meets their specific needs. In order to effectively teach and reach all students, teachers need to know how to find out what their students know and are able to do (through formative/summative assessment) and apply the results of assessments to inform instruction and resource selection. Teaching needs to be responsive, not one-size-fits all, it's an equity issue.

Lageman has continued to follow her passion for assessment literacy by partnering with educators, administrators, and policy makers to support progress and learning growth for all. She serves on the board of the Maryland Assessment Group (MAG).

In 2018 she partnered with Dr. Bonnie Hain, chief of academics and district services at CenterPoint Education Solutions, to present a preconference session at the fall MAG Conference entitled, "Developing a Systemic Assessment Plan: A High-Leverage Strategy for Increasing Student Achievement." Session participants determined the data needed at the system, district, school, and classroom levels; reviewed current systemic assessments available and the degree to which they meet systemic data needs; and verified, clarified, or modified systemic assessment plans.

In her role as chair of the Learning Forward Foundation, Lageman strengthened her commitment to providing opportunities for educators and leaders to learn and grow, and her commitment to formative assessment. The 2018 Learning Forward Foundation Team Grant was awarded to Christina Miller, coordinator of formative assessment in Charles County Public Schools in La Plata, Maryland, and Heather Sauers, coordinator of professional learning and Title IIA at the MSDE.

The goal of the grant is to take FAME to the next level of implementation by creating more robust professional learning processes for teachers and school leadership teams, and more support for educators as they implement formative assessments into their practice. Miller and Sauers used the grant to provide a formative assessment course titled, "Formative Assessment for Leadership Teams" that is research-based, job-embedded, and aimed at supporting changes in teacher practice.

Across all areas of teaching and learning, assessment literacy is a moral obligation, and students have a civil right to an assessment-literate teacher. Exploring the role of assessment literacy in authentic teaching and learning is essential to developing the whole child, and to providing every student with numerous open doors to achieve his or her full learning potential. We know better—now we need to do better and use our networks to build assessment literacy by whatever means possible.

Additional resources:

- Linquanti, Robert. 2014. *Supporting Formative Assessment for Deeper Learning: A Primer for Policymakers.* Washington, DC: Council of Chief State School Officers. https://www.michigan.gov/documents/mde/CCSSO_Supporting_Formative_Assessment_for_Deeper_Learning_601111_7.pdf.
- Brookhart, Susan, and Sheryl Lazarus. 2017. *Formative Assessment for Students with Disabilities.* https://ccsso.org/sites/default/files/2017-12/Formative_Assessment_for_Students_with_Disabilities.pdf.
- How I Know: Designing Meaningful Formative Practice—http://www.formativeassessmentpractice.org

REFLECTION QUESTIONS

1. How might a school or district support the wider use of the formative assessment process by classroom teachers?

2. What type of support from administrators and district offices is needed to promote collaborative practices that support assessment literacy?
3. How might faculties of school(s) work together to provide the needed support to learn about and to use formative assessment practices with their students?

NOTE

1. Originally published in a slightly different form from Formative Assessment for Michigan Educators (FAME) Research and Development Team, *The Hesperia Story: The Focus Is on the Students*, A Case Study: Implementation of the Formative Assessment Process in Michigan (Lansing, MI: FAME, 2019), https://famemichigan.org/wp-content/uploads/2019/06/CaseStudy_Hesperia_6.19.pdf. Reprinted by permission of the publisher.

Chapter 7

Communicate with Students and Families

Kathy S. Dyer, Jacki Ball,
Chadwick Anderson, and Alison Mund

SECTION BY KATHY S. DYER

The impact (and use) of any assessment is a direct function of the effectiveness of how information is communicated to its intended users. Assessments are valuable to both students and their families: they let students demonstrate what they know, determine what they do not know, and make plans for moving forward on their learning path. Families are partners in students' learning; and providing families with information about students' learning allows them to support students outside of the classroom.

Over time, assessment results give learners multiple opportunities to set goals and monitor their growth. The evidence of learning generated by assessments provides teachers useful insights for informed conversations with both learners and families.

Strategies for family engagement vary among schools, but the main idea is to communicate with families early and often. Providing information about the purpose and use of a particular assessment may alleviate stress and answer questions before they even form. Identifying potential barriers to families understanding the various types of assessment used in the school, and particularly in the classroom, may be a starting point.

What do parents need to know and understand about an assessment to see it and the evidence from the assessment as a support for their child's learning? If the primary purpose of assessment is to support learning, then communicating the results of an assessment in ways that are timely, clear, and concise is critical to all stakeholders, particularly students and families (Bonner 2013, 87–106).

Assessment-literate educators know how to communicate information to support student learning. Whether this communication occurs using sound grading practices or conversations with learners about their learning progress, it should happen often. Parents can be partners in students' learning when educators find ways to keep them informed of their children's learning progress, which is one way of building trust in this relationship. Accurately explaining the meaning and appropriate use of results (evidence) from assessments to all stakeholders is a priority for assessment-literate educators.

As evidenced by Jeynes (2005, 237–69), family engagement in school is associated with higher academic achievement across all demographics. When schools and families work together to support learners, students tend to do better (Kraft and Rogers 2015, 49; Bergman and Chan 2019, 2). Encouraging teachers to talk with families about assessment can support this increase in achievement. Talking about the purpose of assessment, explaining a learner's progress, and identifying academic and nonacademic strengths and areas for growth empower family members by giving them meaningful information they can use to better support learning at school and home. Communicating about assessment evidence with families can be part of the trust building that occurs in the relationship between home and school.

Berger et al. (2014, 2) describe student-engaged assessment as "a system of interrelated practices that positions students as leaders of their own learning." Communication is a key practice in this system. From the communication of the learning targets and success criteria to learners setting goals—through the giving, making sense, and using of learning-focused feedback to monitor the progress of their learning—students are constantly communicating about what they know, what they do not know, and how they plan to fill in gaps or move ahead. In school, student-led conferences provide a mechanism for sharing this information with families.

Student-Led Conferences

Since the early 2000s, student-led conferences have made inroads into the traditional parent-teacher conference scene. When a student leads a conference, they use (and develops) a multitude of metacognitive skills, all necessary for success in school. Furthermore, providing learners the opportunity to engage in student-led conferences gives them an authentic purpose for developing many skills necessary for success in college and careers.

Through the preparation process, students reflect on themselves and their journey as learners, and they build a sense of accountability and responsibility for learning. To identify which examples of their work they will present, students develop a deeper understanding of what it means to meet success criteria. They must also establish a process to make decisions regarding work to share and what to say about that work—a way to justify their conclusions about their own learning. They become a self-advocate when it comes to learning.

Flipping conferences to be student-led facilitates a partnership between the teacher and family members focused on supporting what the student identifies as his or her strengths and challenges in learning. It offers an opportunity to enhance family engagement in learning, in many places showing an increase in parent participation (Richmond 2016).

What if the conversation became more about student learning, student strengths, and needs, and less about explaining or defending grades? What if one of the potential aftereffects included an increase in learner-family communication with an extra benefit that the conversations would be focused on academics, rather than on how the day went?

In 2016 Gallup and Northwest Evaluation Association (NWEA) partnered to survey educators, students, and parents about communicating assessment results. One finding was startling—61 percent of surveyed parents said their child's teacher rarely or never discussed their child's assessment results with them.

This finding tells us there is more need to communicate with families when it comes to assessment—about both the results the assessments produce and how their children's teachers use those results to advance learning. Parents surveyed considered multiple types of assessments, including interim and formative assessments, helpful to their children's learning. Findings from this survey reinforce the idea that depending on the school's population and environment, teachers may encounter challenges when trying to engage parents about their learners' assessment evidence.

The National Assessment Governing Board (2012, 3) reminds us that "parents are the primary advocates for the quality of their children's education. Having solid information about education achievement improves their ability to advocate and ask the right questions." Providing families critical information about student learning early and often should include verification of understanding of the connection between the evidence of learning, the pending instructional decisions, and student learning activities.

Learners' assessment results tell a story. Frequently the elements of that story omit more formal methods of decision-making (Pink 2005, 103). The personal communication on where learners are in their learning path, and how the assessment evidence can support them in getting to where they either want or need to be, can be a powerful component in the learning journey of students and their families.

Harvard Family Research Project (2013, 4–8) provides several practical recommendations for school leaders and teachers to share student data on a regular basis and in meaningful ways to strengthen family-school partnerships. For example, it is important to provide parents with a brief definition or explanation of data that have been sent home or posted on an online parent portal. Educators should avoid as much education jargon as possible (e.g., acronyms or terms such as "formative") and work to create a glossary of commonly used words to help families understand assessment and performance-related terms that they are likely to see in print and online.

Additionally, educators should approach sharing data with families in the context of the whole child. A student's progress is more than the sum of test scores or attendance records. Teachers should be ready to supplement such information with daily classroom observations and maybe include social and problem-solving skills and contributions to class discussions. Also, be sensitive to the diverse cultural and linguistic backgrounds of families and recognize that these can influence the ways that you interact with them.

Finally, give families agency. Educators do not need to provide all the data or answers to student learning issues—invite families to share their own observations of their child to make them active partners with whom you share a clear objective. Families should leave with resources (e.g., websites, activities, open source materials, afterschool programs) most relevant to their child's needs and to enrich their child's learning.

While the conventional way educators share assessment results with families is through parent-teacher conferences, these opportunities typically do not occur often enough to foster ongoing school-family communication and information sharing. However, teachers are becoming more proactive in how they communicate with families, and many share information in between report cards and conferences (Harvard Family Research Project 2013, 2). Parents are also asking more questions about the assessment data to better understand their child's learning.

Taken together, such actions allow families and educators to engage in intentional discussions about student progress more frequently than in the past and build a sense of shared responsibility for supporting student learning. Equipped with new technology tools and platforms, educators and families can stay connected in exciting new ways. We first hear from Jacki Ball from National PTA who offers some recommendations for educators about communicating assessment results with families and parents. We then turn to Westminster Public Schools (WPS) in Colorado to learn more about how teachers implemented a robust competency-based system (CBS) that keeps students and families updated.

CASE STUDY BY JACKI BALL

Strengthening School-Family Partnerships: National PTA Recommendations

Parents and their children are the consumers of our nation's public education system, and parents are essential partners in education. However, they have not always been included at the decision-making table and considered as critical collaborators with teachers in their child's education experience. This exclusion has caused confusion, mistrust, and criticism when initiatives such as new assessments have been considered and implemented. Without consistent, ongoing engagement and two-way meaningful communication, parents, families, and students feel that education is being done to them instead of coexisting as equals in their educational journey.

National PTA believes building successful partnerships starts with the National Standards for Family-School Partnerships (National PTA 2019). The six standards address elements for successful family-school partnerships that support student success. These standards include welcoming all families, having meaningful two-way communication, supporting student success, speaking up for every child, sharing power, and collaborating with the community. Schools and educators should embrace these standards as common practice to engage families.

In recent years, there has arguably been an overemphasis on testing, which has resulted in "teaching only to the test" and "narrowing down" the curriculum—activities that place a burden on classroom time and deny students a full educational experience. Test scores have also been inappropriately used as a single metric of student achievement, teacher effectiveness, and school success (Bay and Monell 2016). This has created frustration and mistrust among some parents and families about the use of assessments. Yet high-quality assessments play an important role in promoting equity, providing parents, teachers, and school leaders with valuable information about student growth and achievement and improving outcomes for all children.

Parents want a fuller picture of their child's learning environment. Research conducted by Learning Heroes (2017) in collaboration with Edge Research, Tembo, and HCM Strategists found that parents value both academic and nonacademic measures. In addition to communicating about assessment results effectively, it is also important for educators to provide other types of meaningful data to families about their child's progress such as attendance, discipline, social interactions, learning environment, and access to experienced teachers (Learning Heroes 2017).

While there are multiple elements to building strong family-school partnerships, communication is the cornerstone. The elements of any cohesive communications strategy to engage families must be transparent, provide high-quality information that is accessible, and include timely feedback and ongoing engagement. These elements build the circle of trust that is necessary for an effective and productive family-school partnership.

Transparency and Trust

Parents and families need to know and understand the assessment and accountability system in place at their child's school. Families must be notified through multiple communication vehicles, such as in-person meetings, digital communications, and print materials, and at regular intervals. Educators should inform parents of required assessments, their purpose, when they will occur, the testing environment, and when results will be available. Additionally, families need to receive information on how educators will use formative and summative assessment data to improve teaching and learning and how they, as their child's first teacher, can use assessment results to support their child's academic growth and achievement.

Experienced principal Aaron Selekman, from Wilmington, Delaware, builds trust with parents and families by holding meetings within the community to engage as many families as possible. Instead of holding three to four parent meetings at the school throughout the year with a large number of attendees, Selekman hosts more frequent events with a smaller number of parents to personalize conversations and create meaningful two-way communication between the school and families. These meetings take place at locations where he can reach parents instead of asking them to come to the school.

Understanding the importance of "meeting parents and families where they are," especially when addressing curriculum, instruction, and assessments, Selekman knows hubs of the community are ideal gathering places for these conversations with students, parents, and families. Thus, Selekman holds meetings around Wilmington at the West End Neighborhood House, the William "Hicks" Anderson Community Center, local churches, the Wilmington Public Library, and the 4th Street McDonald's.

As a principal at Anna P. Mote Elementary School, Henry B. du Pont (H.B.) Middle School, and now Newark High School, Selekman has encouraged other educators to listen carefully to identify parent and family concern(s) and then explicitly address them in conversations with families. In personalized conversations with parents on assessments, he provides information based on student needs and angst.

For instance, Selekman hosts meetings for parents of students with 504 plans or Individualized Education Plans (IEPs), parents of students with test anxiety, and parents of English language learners. Instead of providing sample questions or reading passages a student might encounter on an assessment, Selekman focuses on the testing environment, explains the accommodations available, and introduces families and students to the proctors.

He found by addressing the needs and concerns of students regarding the learning environment students would have before, during, and after assessments, fewer parents were resistant to state assessments and more inclined to have their children participate in them. Numerous families who originally opted their child out of Delaware's state tests changed their minds after meeting with Selekman or attending a community meeting. Through direct and transparent engagement with families on the value and use of assessment and the testing environment students' experience, Selekman has seen student participation rates and student achievement increase at each school under his leadership.

High-Quality, Family-Friendly Information

Most parents are not experts on assessments, but they are experts on their own children. Parents are their child's first teacher and want to continue to support their child through their educational journey. It is important that information about assessments be explained in simple terms. Information should be accessible and in terms parents can understand; they need to be able to answer important questions such as, "How will this assessment impact my child? Impact my child's education and the school? What information does it provide about my child's progress toward grade-level and college-and-career readiness?"

Information should be disseminated to families using multiple means (e.g., digitally, in person, through printed copies sent home) and not hidden in the depths of a website.

Written materials should be clear and concise. Most parents do not have the time to spend dissecting charts and graphs or reading lengthy paragraphs. The information provided to parents needs to answer the essential question, "What information on assessments is most meaningful and important for helping them support their child's learning?"

Keeping information short and simple is critical for parents. For example, a parent in California shares his or her perspective on reading a school report card that included assessment results: "It was really lengthy—lots of scales and charts and paragraphs. I think I started reading, then glanced at the rest and then said I'll go back to it and just never did. It just felt like I didn't have time to read the whole thing" (Learning Heroes 2017).

National PTA recommends that family-friendly resources should be no longer than three written pages, preferably one to two pages that are visually appealing and easy to read. Effective materials for parents should also include contextual cover letters or information that explains what the assessment measures and how the results can be used to support student learning and that lists recommended strategies that parents can do at home with their child.

For example, the Ohio Department of Education (ODE) produces an interpretive guide for families on each Ohio state test to assist parents in understanding the information provided in score reports. The interpretative guides, which reflect the report a family will receive, are short in length, nicely designed, and easily digestible. They include callout boxes that clearly describe important elements of the score report that a parent can use to more easily interpret the data. The score reports give a clear visualization of students' performance levels, what their results mean, and the next steps parents can take to support their child's learning. Additionally, the score report provides a glossary of terms and a frequently-asked-questions section (Ohio Department of Education 2019).

To assist schools and educators in providing high-quality and parent-friendly information on assessments, states, school districts, and schools should partner with their state and local PTAs to develop and disseminate family-friendly resources. PTAs can offer helpful input and feedback (including drafting and reviewing) on score reports and other assessment-related information for parents. Additionally, PTA and other community-based organizations can act as trusted messengers to disseminate information about assessments to parents and families and cohost meetings with educators to discuss assessments and results.

An example of leveraging parent voice to improve communications on assessments and college- and career-readiness occurred in West Virginia. The West Virginia Department of Education (WVDE) reached out to West Virginia PTA to solicit parents to participate in the Community Engagement Advisory Council to improve the WVDE's digital and printed communications.

The WVDE purposefully engaged a variety of stakeholders from all over the state, including educators and community-based organizations. Specifically, parents asked the WVDE to provide clearer explanations and simple graphs with distinguishable color variance on the individual student score report that enable parents, guardians, and caregivers (such as grandparents) to understand whether their child is meeting grade-level standards.

Additionally, stakeholders wanted to make sure assessment reports were crafted and designed so that high school students could read and understand their results as well.

The WVDOE worked with its testing vendor for third through eighth grades, American Institutes for Research (AIR), to simplify the individual student assessment reports to show a bar graph that clearly illustrates students' overall performance in the areas of English language arts (ELA), math, and science. Students in third through eighth grades receive a four-page, full-color report that includes their performance in ELA and math, while students in grades five and eight receive a two-page, full-color report for science. Figure 7.1 is a sample of the science report.

All individual student reports include a contextual overview from the state superintendent on the importance and value of the assessment and what results show about student performance. The results also include next steps parents can take to support their child's learning at home. West Virginia students in eleventh grade take the SAT School Day as the state's annual

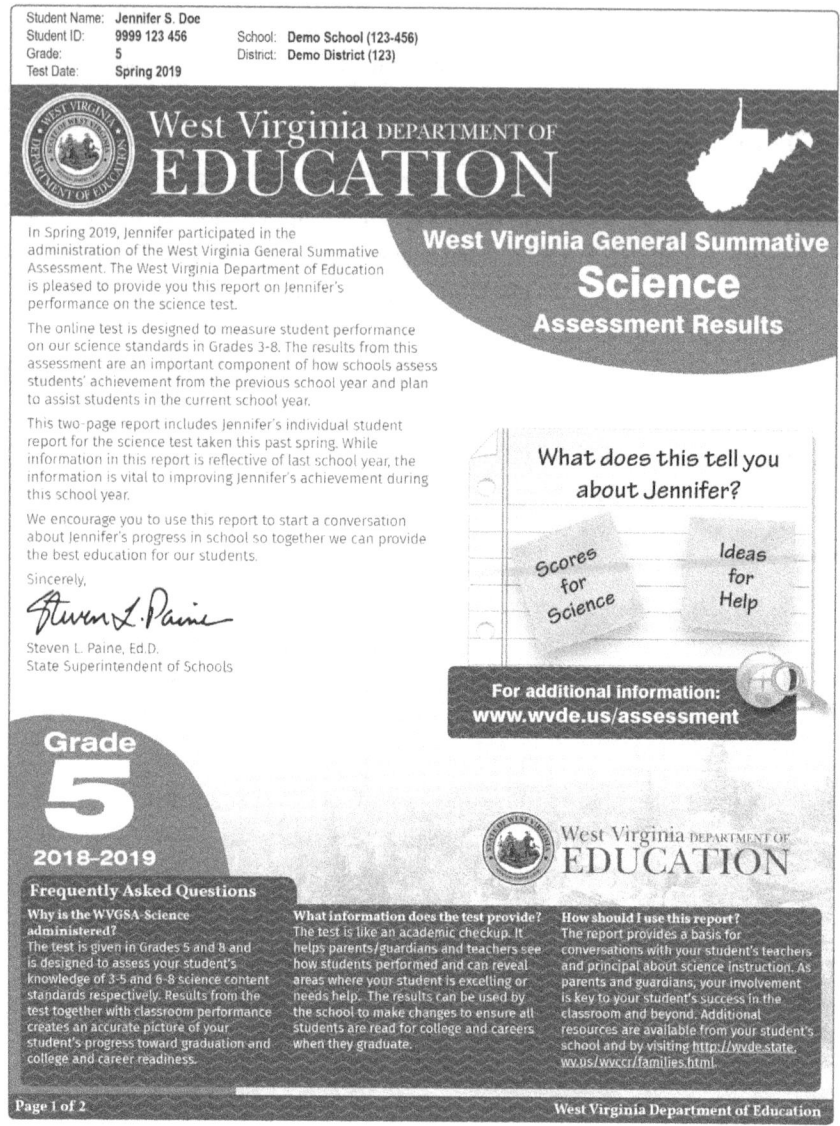

Figure 7.1 West Virginia General Summative Science Assessment Results. West Virginia Department of Education.

summative assessment. Although these students receive a standard SAT report, the WVDE also designed its own customized parent report similar to the one provided for students in third through eighth grades.

Producing family-friendly materials also means attending to the reading level used to describe student's performance. The Data Quality Campaign

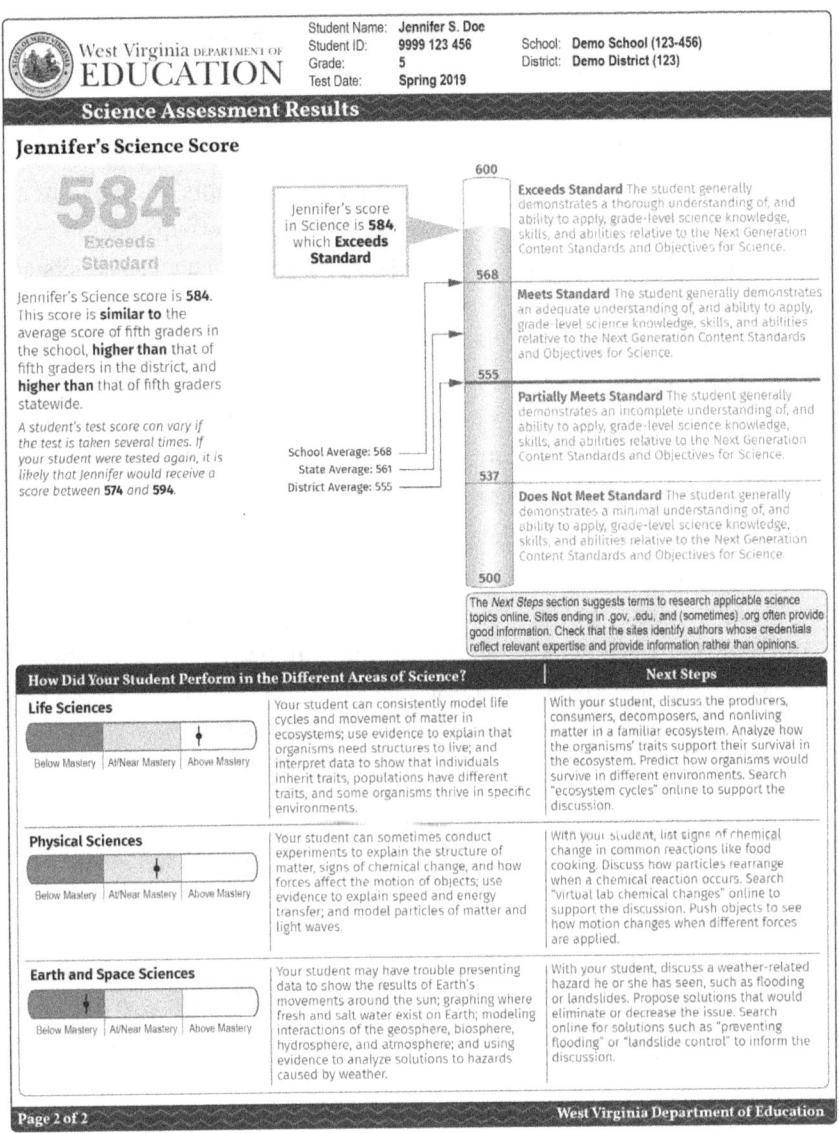

Figure 7.1 Continued

(2019) found in an analysis of state report cards that the average text on a report card is at a college level when best practice is to write content at a reading level not greater than the eighth grade.

West Virginia's science assessment results include text that scores on a readability scale from grade level third to tenth. For example, the explanation of this student's science score is at a third-grade level, the description of her performance on Earth and space sciences is at a seventh-grade level, and the definition of *Meets Standard* is at a tenth-grade level.

During the stakeholder engagement forum, a parent shared their perspective on assessment results, which is important for educators to keep in mind: "You see this every day, but parents don't see this type of information every day. It's needs to be simplified so that a parent and/or student can understand what their results mean."

Educators must also ensure the information delivered is accessible for *all* parents and families, no matter their language. States, districts, and schools must provide translations and translation services, so all families can deeply engage in their child's education. It is essential that assessment-related materials appear in the most used languages other than English in a school community. Using simplified language is key to making sure that translated material is at an appropriate reading level.

Although it takes time and resources, providing this service demonstrates a commitment to making sure all parents and families have the information they need to support their child's learning and development. The Massachusetts Department of Elementary and Secondary Education (DESE) and the Ohio Department of Education (ODE) are leading the way in providing translated material for parents and families.

The DESE translates resources on school and district report cards for families in ten different languages—Arabic, Cape Verdean Creole, Chinese, Haitian Creole, Khmer, Portuguese, Russian, Spanish, and Vietnamese—that are immediately accessible on the home page for these reports. The ODE provides the interpretative guide for Ohio's state tests in eleven languages—Arabic, Chinese, French, German, Japanese, Korean, Russian, Somali, Spanish, Ukrainian, and Vietnamese.

Furthermore, education leaders must provide accommodations for parents and family members with disabilities. Estimates indicate that approximately 4.1 million parents with a disability have school-age children (Through the Looking Glass 2013, 7). Schools should be mindful that a parent's disability might not be obvious, and parents may not be inclined to disclose it. A best practice to engage all parents and families regardless of disability is to ask families their preferred means of communication, which can open dialogue regarding accommodations that may be needed. Taking this approach at the beginning of the school year is a great way to demonstrate commitment to engaging families in their child's education.

Ongoing Engagement with Parents and Families

Systems and structures need to be put into place for parents to provide regular and ongoing input and feedback, and education leaders need to listen when parents share their thoughts regarding their child's education and performance. Parents must have dedicated opportunities to engage with their child's teachers on assessment results, be able to ask questions, and understand how they can use the information to better support their child's education.

The Rhode Island Department of Education (RIDE) identifies three important types of data conversations:

- gathering information;
- guiding improvement;
- finding solutions.

To assist in these conversations, RIDE provides recommendations for educators on how to engage in these discussions with parents, students, and colleagues through positive presumptions, paraphrasing, planning, and questioning techniques and exercises to enhance data-driven dialogue (Rhode Island Department of Education and Amplify Education, Inc. 2013).

Educators can also look to *Toolkit of Resources for Engaging Families and the Community as Partners in Education: Part 4: Engaging All in Data Conversations* (Garcia et al. 2016), which provides useful activities for teachers to hone their skills to better engage families on student achievement, including utilizing assessment results in meaningful ways. The toolkit demonstrates the importance of using positive presumptions and questioning through this example:

> A teacher and a parent are reviewing a student's data related to completion of in-class and homework assignments for math. The parent is concerned that the student has completed very few homework assignments and only half of the in-class assignments. The teacher and parent discuss their views on the importance of homework and how it relates to student learning. They teacher says, "You and I agree that if Maria completes her homework, she is more likely to achieve the math standards for her grade level. What barriers prevent Maria

from consistently doing her homework?" The statement of agreement that completing homework will improve the student's academic performance sets up a baseline for action. The question opens the dialogue about possible reasons that the student does not complete her homework and possible ways to address the issue (Garcia et al. 2016, 31).

While most schools host parent-teacher conferences, schools should consider if these conferences are being leveraged for intentional conversations on assessment data and student performance and what other opportunities exist or need to be created. Intentional conversations on assessment and student performance should provide parents and educators the chance to review and reflect on academic and nonacademic data, discuss student strengths, interests, and challenges and offer parents the opportunity to provide feedback on the usefulness of the information they are receiving.

For example, Learning Heroes developed *From Puzzle to Plan: A Family Worksheet* that allows for a meaningful conversation among the student, family, and teacher regarding student performance. The worksheet also encourages dialogue on student motivation and challenges and provides links to resources to support learning at home (Learning Heroes 2018). Parents overwhelmingly praise *A Family Worksheet*. A parent from Cincinnati sums up the positive feedback this way: "I would feel like there was a partnership between me and the teacher. We're both working on. Now we have a plan. I love it. I want a copy of this. I like having a plan and I think my son would like it" (Learning Heroes 2018, 23).

Educational leaders must also consider the need for professional development and other supports that empower teachers to effectively engage families in assessment conversations. All teachers in the school building should be using a shared language to communicate with families on assessments. At Grant High School in Portland, Oregon, the school employs a data coordinator who works with language arts and math teachers to review and analyze assessment data and provides in-service professional development to classroom teachers on effective communication with parents and families.

While some schools and districts provide professional development to support data-driven conversations within the school and with parents, schools of education should ensure that preservice teachers are able to interpret assessment data and communicate it to parents and families and effectively engage families in their child's education.

Parents want specific recommendations and regular communication on how to support their child's learning based on their current performance and progress. At Grant High School, the first parent-teacher conference of the year includes a discussion with parents on their child's performance on last year's state assessment, areas for growth, and what standards should be met by the end of the school year.

Subsequent parent-teacher conferences at Grant address current progress and performance and whether the student is on track to meet the grade-level standards. Then, before the start of the state assessment window, the English and math departments hold grade-level open houses to give parents and families specific information on the state assessment and current student progress related to standards.

From the viewpoint of a parent, a parent-teacher conference is successful when parents can walk away with actionable steps they can take to support their child. For example, a parent in Oregon shared the following observation:

> The most remarkable parent-teacher conference I ever had for my son, Thomas, was with Ms. Kelly at Alameda Elementary School. My son was struggling with addition and Ms. Kelly provided me with a card game I could play at home with Thomas to help him improve. Ms. Kelly used information from formative assessments to provide parents with specific recommendations based on the child's needs and current performance to grade level standards.

Parent-teacher conferences should not focus solely on how a child is currently performing in a specific classroom. These conversations should also include a review of overall student assessment performances, student growth, and academic and nonacademic measures of student achievement.

For these conversations to be even more meaningful to families and educators, assessment results must be timely. It is a disservice to students, parents, and educators when they receive assessment data past its usefulness to improve teaching and learning. States have made progress in improving the dissemination of score reports, but there is still room for growth. While improvements continue to be made in this area, classroom educators can learn from Ms. Kelly and seek to incorporate relevant formative and previous summative assessment results as they engage and collaborate with families in service of student learning.

Additional Resources: One tool to assess whether the information provided will be understandable to most parents is to use the Hemingway App, a free online tool that evaluates a text's grade level and sentence structure.

CASE STUDY BY CHADWICK ANDERSON AND ALISON MUND

Empowering Students: How Westminster Public Schools (WPS) Communicate Assessment Results

Student agency. It is a buzz word heard everywhere educators gather. Education is not a thing to be done *to* students; it is something to be done *with* students. Creating opportunities for students to own their individual learning aspirations and trajectories and helping them be aware early on of the skills and knowledge they will need is the cornerstone of a competency-based, learner-centered approach to schooling that educational reformers say is needed within our field.

Westminster Public Schools (WPS), in the metropolitan area of Denver, Colorado, implemented a learner-centered, CBS of education a decade ago and has been refining it every year. "Where Education is Personal" is the tagline for this urban district of almost ten thousand students taught in twenty schools. Seventy-six percent of WPS students are Latino/Hispanic, 39 percent are English language learners, and 79 percent qualify for free or reduced-priced lunch. There is a 20 percent mobility rate in the student population.

The WPS CBS recognizes that all children are different, and their learning should be personalized so they are engaged and involved every step of the way. Instead of students being grouped by age, they are grouped by demonstrated performance level. Students who are ready for more challenging content move to the next level without delay, while those who need extra help receive it in a timely manner. CBS requires students to show mastery of learning targets before moving on to the next level. This approach allows some students to progress more quickly, while others may take more time to fill in their gaps in learning.

WPS challenges the ineffective practice of social promotion, which historically has allowed lower-performing students to "squeak by" with a D- while lacking the skills and competencies needed to be successful after graduation.

Student agency within such a CBS is essential. Rather than being passive recipients of knowledge transfer, learners take the driver's seat, plotting a logical and self-chosen course through clearly delineated learning targets within a series of performance levels leading to graduation.

This educational reform is gaining traction nationwide because it is best for kids and families. It is imperative that school children be involved in charting their educational journeys while being accountable for demonstrating competency in the necessary skills to be ready for the next level of learning.[1]

Clear and explicit presentation of student learning outcomes (SLOs), termed *learning targets* in the district, is necessary to promote student agency. At every level and in every classroom, teachers are trained to begin lessons and units of study by ensuring student understanding of what skills and knowledge will be attained. Further, learning targets are posted, referenced, and reviewed throughout the lesson and checked back on for formative lesson closure.

Student agency means it is the students' job to check their work against the clearly defined success criteria and reflect on whether they are successful or what they need to do to show proficiency. Sound assessment practices guide this process as teachers and students check in on individual goals and weigh student work and skills against success criteria.

Reporting, Recording, and Trainings

Empower, a dynamic digit reporting and recording system, is used by WPS teachers, students, and parents. It allows teachers to record student progress and communicate with both parents and students quickly. Teachers use this tool to mark progress toward proficiency on WPS scales. It is updated weekly, so the most accurate data are available. Students have 24-7 access to Empower, and they can see exactly what they have accomplished and what work they need to finish.

In the tool, teachers can create playlists containing all the necessary resources and assignments students need to complete to show proficiency. This gives students the freedom to work through proficiency scales independently and at their own productive pace. Playlists are also helpful when looking to fill gaps students might have in their learning. Finally, Empower can send updates to parents regarding late and missing assignments. Having a flexible and comprehensive reporting and recording system is an essential component to the district's CBS.

Communicating student learning outcomes and academic progress to parents is vital in creating and maintaining a healthy home-school partnership. For parents to properly understand Empower and be able to navigate effectively within the online system, some face-to-face training is needed.

Resource trainings are frequently offered in schools during back-to-school nights, parent-teacher conferences, literacy nights, math nights, and other community events. School-level personnel such as counselors, community education specialists, instructional coaches, office staff, and teachers are available to sit down with parents and show them how to use the tool. WPS also offers many online and printable resources, available in Spanish and English, to support parents.

Alpine

WPS uses Alpine Achievement to house local, as well as state-level, student assessment data. This online system allows educators to view snapshots of individual student assessment results on a wide variety of assessments including the Colorado Measures of Academic Success (CMAS), WIDA ACCESS, Scantron Performance Series, CBS Performance Level Placement, and PSAT.

Alpine also allows educators to create custom rosters and dashboards to view progress over time on multiple assessment instruments, to compare disaggregated student groups, and to triangulate multiple data sources to create real-time bodies of evidence. This system is a far more modern and user-friendly tool than the traditional data spreadsheet and allows educators to have a wealth of student data at their fingertips. With this resource, Westminster teachers can use online data to inform instructional decisions in a quick and efficient manner.

Student Agency

In the WPS CBS, the importance of student agency cannot be overstated. Students must take ownership of their learning. To support students in this important task, teachers have them track their progress, create goals, develop a plan for meeting these goals, evaluate the outcome, and make adjustments to reach success. The use of data notebooks is a huge component of this process.

Each student has a data notebook that houses important information regarding their progress and next steps. A Competency Tracker is used for students to monitor the level at which they are currently performing in the various content areas. A Student Data Picture shows the various state and district assessments students have taken and what their proficiently level is for those assessments. Both tools allow students to set appropriate, personalized goals. Additional information, such as formative assessment information, is included in these data notebooks to help students build on strengths, set specific goals, and monitor their progress.

Goal-setting sheets are another key component of the data notebooks. These help students work through the process of setting a specific, measurable, and attainable goal. It includes creating a plan for how the student will accomplish this goal as well as a timeline. Additionally, the timeline contains opportunities to check on the progress being made and, if appropriate, to see what adjustments were made to meet the goal. When students know what they need to do, are involved in tracking their progress, have a voice, are given choices, and understand what success looks like, they begin to take agency in their own learning.

Community Outreach

Community Education Specialists

WPS families are diverse, representing forty world languages and a myriad of cultures. Forming partnerships with the families and keep them well informed not only of their students' academic progress but also of school and community events and noteworthy occurrences are high priorities for the school district.

To this end, each school employs a community education specialist. This classified position is a resource for the school community and provides Empower training, educates and informs parents and community members about the CBS system, conducts English classes, and facilitates volunteerism and parent leadership. All WPS community education specialists are bilingual in Spanish and English and are trained in the systems and resources to support families in ensuring their children's success in school and beyond.

Parent Academy for Student Success

Another rich and informative resource that WPS offers its parent community is the Parent Academy for Student Success (PASS) program. PASS is a free program open to all WPS parents, including Spanish speakers. PASS helps parents open the door to opportunity for their children. Hosted each semester at a different WPS site, the program focus is postsecondary readiness, and within that context PASS informs and educates parents regarding district systems and resources. PASS participants are committed to helping their sons and daughters to be ready for life after high school.

PASS has been offered in three middle and high schools, graduating over 250 parents and positively impacting over 600 of their students in their quest to pursue higher education. Because of the PASS program, WPS has seen a definite uptick in parental leadership and involvement in our school district. The common knowledge base provided by PASS is particularly helpful in communicating with families regarding their students' educational progress.

Instructional Coaches

Instructional coaches help forge great partnerships between parents and Westminster schools. Some schools have instructional coaches who work onsite, while other instructional coaches are assigned at the district level and work in multiple schools. Instructional coaches are invaluable resources for providing support and training to teachers, both new and veteran staff. Instructional coaches go into classrooms to provide whatever support is needed, including modeling, co-teaching, observing and providing feedback, locating and providing resources, and supporting the teacher in planning. Just like the personalized learning WPS provides its students, instructional coaches help individualize the support the district offers to teachers and families.

Communication of High-Stakes Assessment Results

Colorado public school students in grades three through eight are required to take CMAS, and high school students are required to take the SAT or PSAT, as well as CMAS Science in the eleventh grade. These are the "high-stakes" summative assessments used ostensibly to certify that learning has taken place. These instruments are also used for accountability purposes in ranking schools and districts to determine how they are performing. Additionally, in conjunction with the state teacher evaluation tool in Colorado, high-stakes assessment results are used as part of a formula to determine teacher effectiveness.

In communicating results to parents, the school mails parents hard copies of individual CMAS and (P)SAT results along with an externally generated form letter explaining, in very general terms, how to interpret the results. During parent-teacher conferences, educators present WPS high-stakes assessment results, as well as results from local measures (e.g., Empower data and formative assessment information) to parents as a body of evidence to certify learning. More importantly, this information is used to identify a clear and data-informed pathway for future learning and ultimately to the all-important day after high school graduation. The Colorado Department of Education has also created an online data center for parents to access information.

Purposeful Strategies That Empower Student and Families

Like all school districts, WPS conducts parent-teacher conferences. They are unique in that students lead these critical discussions and help share their information. Many schools use a student-led format to conduct parent-teacher conferences. These should really be called *student-parent conferences*, as the students are responsible for sharing where they are academically, their strengths, the goals they have set for themselves within the competency tracker, how they plan to achieve these goals, and the support they may need to be successful. This is the ultimate expression of student agency. When students share this information with their parents and can answer specific questions regarding their education, they are truly in control of their educational destiny.

Challenges and Conclusions

Implementing a CBS is not without challenges. Early on, WPS learned that an even distribution of learning targets across performance levels was needed so students did not feel stuck in one performance level for too long. WPS also adjusted its levels from fourteen to ten to twelve to more closely match grade-level patterns and to more easily describe students' progress with relation to their chronological age. Maintaining this system requires a robust, dynamic, and flexible method of recording and reporting. The district's Empower system has undergone multiple improvement iterations to match student and teacher needs.

Communicating to parents, the community, and institutions of higher learning about the differences between the CBS system and more traditional approaches has been challenging. Deep-seeded assumptions based on personal experiences about schooling cause people outside WPS to misunderstand the depth of this educational reform. Additionally, helping colleges and universities embrace the WPS use of a competency-based transcript has led to frequent conversation between guidance counselors and representatives from higher education. In spite of these challenges, WPS has stayed the course for the last decade and continues to champion its CBS.

WPS and its CBS are at the forefront of public education reform nationwide. With the implementation of a cutting-edge and learner-centered approach to schooling, supported by best practices for formative assessment, and the use of a data management system that engages and informs parents and students, WPS has changed the discussion about what personalized learning can and should be. WPS educators are pleased with its ever-improving outcomes for students and are honored to serve its community of diverse learners.

REFLECTION QUESTIONS

1. How are you providing the most important and relevant assessment information and data to parents and families?
2. How are you providing information to parents and families that they can easily understand and use to support their child's learning and growth?
3. Can you identify unique opportunities to engage with parents and families alongside traditional family nights and parent-teacher conferences?

NOTE

1. To learn more about the WPS CBS, visit https://www.westminsterpublicschools.org/cbswps.

Conclusion

Across the country, educators are using assessments to support equitable learning opportunities. Among different roles in various organizations throughout the nation, assessment data have been analyzed with an eye toward tailoring instruction to meet students' needs. Each chapter bridges research and theory with practical applications at the district, school, and classroom levels. In the introduction, you were introduced to three myths about assessment. The chapters in the book provided examples that combat these myths. Below, themes from the chapters are organized under each myth as a way to show that there are a range of ways to enact strategies to use assessment to support student learning and advance equitable outcomes.

MYTH 1: ASSESSMENTS JUST LET YOU KNOW IF YOU GET IT OR NOT

Truth 1: Assessments are a tool that can be used to support learning.

While one purpose of assessments is to communicate whether students have absorbed the content taught, assessments have multiple purposes. Chapter 5 provides a framework for thinking through who uses assessments, how the results will be used, and what information or evidence is needed. The primary purpose of assessment should be to support learning, and as the case studies demonstrate, this occurs in a variety of ways.

First, well-constructed assessments provide a concrete description of what it looks like when students understand and are able to apply the content taught. In this way, a critical part of formative assessment includes the practice of clarifying and sharing learning targets, as noted in the introduction in the statement from the Council of Chief State School Officers (CCSSO) (2018, 1–2). In classrooms that have a formative assessment culture, teachers and students come to a shared understanding of the goals of learning, and what is needed to demonstrate that students have met the learning target.

To ensure that students understood what they were supposed to know and be able to do after each lesson, the principal of a rural high school in North Carolina provided teachers with professional development (see chapter 5). At National University in San Diego, faculty support teacher candidates completing a specialization in assessment literacy by creating sound learning targets to ensure that instruction, assessment, and feedback are aligned. As seen in chapter 4, this alignment allows teachers to gather evidence of whether their teaching has resulted in the desired learning and enables students to use the feedback to make progress toward the goal.

Second, assessment results communicate important information to a variety of stakeholders. Authentic, timely communication with the people being assessed or with other stakeholders regarding what the assessment data mean is listed as one of the four primary considerations of a purposeful assessment system in chapter 5. In their case study of novice teachers in chapter 2, Dr. Susan Nolen and Dr. Susan Cooper give the example of using a course grade created in a classroom context to communicate some form of competency to groups such as students, their parents, their future teachers, and college admissions boards.

And of course, parents will want to know about their child's progress in school. As seen in chapter 7, the West Virginia Department of Education (WVDE) partnered with the state Parent Teacher Association to develop clearer explanations and graphs on the individual student score report to enable parents and guardians to understand whether their child is meeting grade-level standards.

Finally, but perhaps most importantly, assessments can be a valuable tool to improve the quality of classroom instruction. Chapter 3's case studies demonstrate how assessments support equitable learning opportunities by informing teachers' decision making and instructional practices.

A physics teacher in a high school outside of Chicago piloted an assessment card system that he used to identify strengths and weaknesses, determine what to teach, adjust lesson pacing, make grouping decisions, empower students to set goals, and support students' educational needs. As a result, the students in his class used learning supports at a higher rate, and he was able to make minor adjustments throughout the year to ensure students achieved goals.

In Kentucky, a reading intervention teacher drew on principles of cognitive science to design an assessment system that enhanced learning. She used opening activities as a form of retrieval practice, requiring students to recall what they had learned in earlier lessons, and spaced out the retrieval practice activities to maximize retention of the skills and strategies taught.

Several chapters touched on the contextual factors that support the use of assessments to improve teaching. Providing time for educators to meet in professional learning communities can facilitate a shared understanding of how students can demonstrate that they have met learning targets, dissemination of best practices in formative assessment to inform mid-lesson shifts in teaching practice, and collaborative efforts to identify instructional strategies to improve student learning.

For example, chapter 6 describes how the superintendent in Hesperia, Michigan, brought principals and teachers together to engage in a Formative Assessment for Michigan Educators (FAME) Learning Team. In Rio Rancho, New Mexico, district leaders supported the use of everyday data to support instructional improvements, illustrated in chapter 1. These collaborative efforts are valued not just for the skill-building that occurs but also because these interactions facilitate trust between educators at different levels of the educational system.

MYTH 2: ASSESSMENTS ARE JUST TESTS

Truth 2: Assessments include a variety of different types of evidence of where students are with regard to learning goals.

While people often think of paper-and-pencil quizzes or end-of-year state exams when they hear "assessment," assessment can take many forms. Chapter 1 explains that in The Center of School District Five of Lexington and Richland Counties, assessments take the form of an individualized capstone project focused on developing potential solutions to a real-world problem and certification tests. Exit slips, thumbs up or thumbs down, and strategic questioning are all examples of assessments that might be embedded throughout a lesson. Some assessments are intended to provide evidence of learning at certain points in time, such as school report card grades, end-of-course tests, the ACT test, and Advanced Placement (AP) exams.

Chapter 2 offers evidence that when novice teachers negotiated assessment practices in their initial teaching placements, they sometimes found that the group projects, portfolios, or performances valued in their teacher preparation programs were overshadowed by an emphasis on quizzes, midterms, and final exams. Several new teachers mentioned the value of rubrics in producing useful information, and others used informal observations of student responses to think-aloud protocols to inform assessment.

While annual state assessments loom large, some educational agencies have devoted considerable attention to other types of assessment as well. Chapter 1 discusses the approach used in Rio Rancho, New Mexico, where the district hired a data coach to help school teams identify what evidence, such as student work or observations of teaching, is necessary to address the question of interest. Teachers at Sandia Vista Elementary School examine sample work from everyday instructional assignments to identify trends and gaps in the students' understanding both within and across the classrooms at their grade level.

Chapter 6 presents examples from both Maryland and Michigan of how state departments of education have launched initiatives that position formative assessment as an essential component of high-quality teaching and learning. In Maryland, this work has been extended to the development of a formative assessment course for leadership teams, aimed at supporting changes in instructional practice.

MYTH 3: ASSESSMENTS ARE JUST USED BY TEACHERS AND ADMINISTRATORS

Truth 3: Assessments are useful for students and parents as well as teachers and administrators.

Assessments and strategies for preparing for assessments help students take ownership of their learning. Both case studies in chapter 3 demonstrate how teachers facilitate this use of assessments. For example, in Kentucky, students in a reading intervention class learn and apply principles of cognitive science to help them retain information. Outside Chicago, students in a physics class use assessment cards to convey what they have learned, what questions they still have, and what additional instructional support they need. In this way, assessments serve as "tools that motivate all students and promote maximum success for all" (Stiggins 2017, 21–22).

As described in chapter 7, some schools have instituted student-led conferences in place of traditional parent-teacher conferences, in which students have the opportunity to self-reflect on where they are with regard to learning targets and provide evidence to support their thinking. Westminster Public Schools (WPS) in Colorado uses an online data system to provide students 24-7 access to their progress on assignments, as well as data notebooks with tools that allow students to set personalized goals based on assessment results.

According to a 2017 survey, a majority of parents said their child's teacher rarely or never discussed their child's assessment results with them, which is a missed opportunity (Gallup and Northwest Evaluation Association 2017, 30). National PTA encourages two-way communication between educators and parents, such as discussion of how families can use assessment results to support their child's academic growth and achievement.

Chapter 7 illustrates how parent-teacher conferences in WPS include a discussion of the results from high-stakes assessment and formative assessments, which are used to identify pathways for future learning. Even light-touch communication about assessments can improve student outcomes; a recent experiment demonstrated that sending parents information on assignments and grades via automated messages reduced course failures (Bergman and Chan 2019, 2).

Assessments can also help stakeholders in different roles and levels of an organization align their efforts toward a common goal. For example, chapter 2 relates how professional learning communities in Omaha, Nebraska, involve teachers in jointly analyzing the work of students, and the leaders who deliver training ask whether teachers have enough time to collaborate and if students have sufficient time with the content.

In this way, assessments are not used *just* by teachers and administrators. Rather, assessments are used by multiple groups of stakeholders with the intent of informing decisions, both at the classroom level for next instructional steps and at the district level to determine what supports teachers need to provide a high-quality learning experience.

As seen in chapter 5, assessments can also help with communicating to stakeholders outside the education system. The principal of the rural high school in North Carolina brought parents, teachers, and community members together in School Improvement Team meetings to discuss what they wanted to know about how students were progressing and what they were learning. Subsequent meetings provided opportunities for stakeholders to learn how to ask students whether they had accomplished their learning goals. As a result, communication between families and schools has increased.

As this volume makes clear, assessments need not be used solely to certify student achievement or sort students into different tracks; assessments also play a powerful role in supporting student learning. Educators can use assessments to better understand their students and to tailor their instructional practices in ways that meet identified needs. The contributors to this volume have shared a variety of ways assessments have been used to support learning at the classroom, school, district, and state levels and have offered insights on the kinds of support educators need in order to be responsive to the information gleaned from assessments. The hope is that these examples will inspire others to support the use of assessments in the classroom in ways that bridge the gap between what is taught and what is learned to ensure more equitable educational opportunities for all students.

References

Allal, Linda. 2010. "Assessment and the Regulation of Learning." In *International Encyclopedia of Education*, edited by Penelope Peterson, Eva Baker, and Barry McGaw, 3rd ed., 348–52. Oxford, England: Elsevier.

Andrade, Heidi, and Susan M. Brookhart. 2016. "The Role of Classroom Assessment in Supporting Self-Regulated Learning." In *Assessment for Learning: Meeting the Challenge of Implementation*, edited by Dany Laveault and Linda Allal, 293–309. Cham, Switzerland: Springer.

Andrade, Heidi L., Ying Du, and Xialei Wang. 2008. "Putting Rubrics to the Test: The Effect of a Model, Criteria Generation, and Rubric-Referenced Self-Assessment on Elementary School Students' Writing." *Educational Measurement: Issues and Practice* 27 (2): 3–13.

Arter, Judith, and Jay McTighe. 2001. *Scoring Rubrics in the Classroom: Using Performance Criteria for Assessing and Improving Student Performance*. Thousand Oaks, CA: Corwin Press.

Ball, Deborah L., and Francesca M. Forzani. 2011. "Building a Common Core for Learning to Teach, and Connecting Professional Learning to Practice." *American Educator* 35 (2): 17–21, 38–39.

Bay, Laura, and Nathan Monell. 2016. Laura Bay and Nathan Monell presentation to PTA Leaders, Members and Supporters, February 11.

Berger, Ron, Leah Rugen, Libby Woodfin, and EL Education. 2014. *Leaders of Their Own Learning: Transforming Schools through Student-Engaged Assessment*. San Francisco: Wiley.

Bergman, Peter, and Eric W. Chan. 2019. "Leveraging Parents through Low-Cost Technology: The Impact of High-Frequency Information on Student Achievement." *The Journal of Human Resources* 54 (3). https://doi.org/10.3368/jhr.56.1.1118-9837R1.

Black, Paul, and Dylan Wiliam. 1998a. "Assessment and Classroom Learning." *Assessment in Education* 5 (1): 7–74.

Black, Paul, and Dylan Wiliam. 1998b. "Inside the Black Box: Raising Standards through Classroom Assessment." *Phi Delta Kapan* 80 (2): 139–48.

Black, Paul, and Dylan Wiliam. 2005. "Changing Teaching through Formative Assessment Research and Practice: The King's-Medway-Oxfordshire Formative Assessment Project." In *Formative Assessment: Improving Learning in Secondary Classrooms*, edited by Centre for Educational Research and Innovation, 223–40. Paris: OECD Publishing.

Black, Paul, and Dylan Wiliam. 2018. "Classroom Assessment and Pedagogy." *Assessment in Education: Principles, Policy & Practice* 25 (6): 551–75.

Black, Paul, Christine Harrison, Clare Lee, Bethan Marshall, and Dylan Wiliam. 2003. *Assessment for Learning Putting it into Practice*. Berkshire, England: Open University Press.

Black, Paul, Christine Harrison, Clare Lee, Bethan Marshall, and Dylan Wiliam. 2014. "Working Inside the Black Box: Assessment for Learning in the Classroom." *The Phi Delta Kappan* 86 (1): 8–21.

Bloom, Benjamin S., ed. 1956. *Taxonomy of Educational Objectives. Vol. 1, Cognitive Domain*. New York: D. McKay.

Bonner, Sarah M. 2013. "Validity in Classroom Assessment: Purposes, Properties, and Principles." In *SAGE Handbook of Research on Classroom Assessment*, edited by James H. McMillan, 87–106. Thousand Oaks, CA: SAGE.

Bowker, Geoffrey C., and Susan Leigh Star. 1999. *Sorting Things Out: Classification and Its Consequences*. Cambridge, MA: MIT Press, 15–16.

Brown, Gavin T. L., and Lois R. Harris. 2013. "Student Self-Assessment." In *SAGE Handbook of Research on Classroom Assessment*, edited by James H. McMillan, 367–94. Thousand Oaks, CA: SAGE.

Chappuis, Jan, Rick Stiggins, Steve Chappius, and Judith A. Arter. 2012. *Classroom Assessment for Student Learning: Doing It Right—Using It Well*. 2nd ed. New York: Pearson.

Coburn, Cynthia E. 2010. "The Partnership for District Change: Challenges of Evidence Use in a Major Urban District." In *Research and Practice in Education: Building Alliances, Bridging the Divide*, edited by Cynthia E. Coburn and Mary Kay Stein, 167–82. Lanham, MD: Rowman & Littlefield.

Coburn, Cynthia E., and Erica O. Turner. 2011. "Research on Data Use: A Framework and Analysis." *Measurement: Interdisciplinary Research & Perspective* 9 (4): 173–206.

Coburn, Cynthia E., Soung Bae, and Erica O. Turner. 2008. "Authority, Status, and the Dynamics of Insider-Outsider Partnerships at the District Level." *Peabody Journal of Education* 83 (3): 364–99.

Cole, Peter. 2004. *Professional Development: A Great Way to Avoid Change*. Seminar Series, no. 140. Jolimont, Victoria: IARTV.

Cooper, Susan E. 2017. "Decisions and Tensions: Summative Assessment in PBL Advanced Placement Classes." PhD diss., University of Washington, Seattle. ProQuest (10288465), 26–41.

Council of Chief State School Officers. 2013. *InTASC Model Core Teaching Standards and Learning Progressions for Teachers 1.0: A Resource for Ongoing Teacher Development*. Washington, DC: Council of Chief State School Officers.

Council of Chief State School Officers. 2018. *Revising the Definition of Formative Assessment*. Washington, DC. https://ccsso.org/resource-library/revising-definition-formative-assessment.

Danielson, Charlotte. 2013. *The Framework for Teaching: Evaluation Instrument*. Princeton, NJ: Danielson Group.

Data Quality Campaign. 2019. *Show Me the Data: States Have Seized the Opportunity to Build Better Report Cards, but the Work Is Not Done*. https://dataqualitycampaign.org/showmethedata.

Datnow, Amanda, and Lea Hubbard. 2016. "Teacher Capacity for and Beliefs about Data-Driven Decision Making: A Literature Review of International Research." *Journal of Educational Change* 17 (1): 7–28.

Datnow, Amanda, Vicki Park, and Brianna Kennedy-Lewis. 2012. "High School Teachers' Use of Data to Inform Instruction." *Journal of Education for Students Placed at Risk (JESPAR)* 17 (4): 247–65.

Downey, Douglas B., David M. Quinn, and Melissa Alcaraz. 2019. "The Distribution of School Quality: Do Schools Serving Mostly White and High-SES Children Produce the Most Learning?" *Sociology of Education* 92 (4): 386–403.

Ebbinghaus, Hermann. 1964. *Memory: A Contribution to Experimental Psychology*. Oxford, England: Dover.

Farley-Ripple, Elizabeth N., and Joan L. Buttram. 2014. "Developing Collaborative Data Use through Professional Learning Communities: Early Lessons from Delaware." *Studies in Educational Evaluation* 42: 41–53.

Gallup, Inc. and Northwest Evaluation Association. 2016. *Make Assessment Work for All Students: Multiple Measures Matter*. Portland, OR: Northwest Evaluation Association. https://www.nwea.org/content/uploads/2016/05/Make_Assessment_Work_for_All_Students_2016.pdf.

Garcia, Maria E., Kay Frunzi, Ceri B. Dean, Nieves Flores, and Kirsten B. Miller. 2016. *Toolkit of Resources for Engaging Families and the Community as Partners in Education: Part 4: Engaging All in Data Conversations*. REL 2016–153. Washington, DC: US Department of Education, Institute of Education Sciences, National Center for Education Evaluation and Regional Assistance, Regional Educational Laboratory Pacific.

Gotwals, Amelia Wenk, and Daniel Birmingham. 2016. "Eliciting, Identifying, Interpreting, and Responding to Students' Ideas: Teacher Candidates' Growth in Formative Assessment Practices." *Research in Science Education* 46 (3): 365–88.

Griffin, Patrick. 2007. "The Comfort of Competence and the Uncertainty of Assessment." *Studies in Educational Evaluation* 33: 87–99.

Grossman, Pamela, Samuel Wineburg, and Stephen Woolworth. 2001. "Toward a Theory of Teacher Community." *Teachers College Record* 103 (6): 942–1012.

Harris, Elizabeth A. 2018. "Chancellor Opposes 'Opt Out' Movement." *New York Times*, April 11. https://www.nytimes.com/2018/04/10/nyregion/tests-chancellor-carranza-nyc-opt-out.html.

Harvard Family Research Project. 2013. *Tips for Administrators, Teachers, and Families: How to Share Data Effectively*. Cambridge, MA: Harvard University Graduate School of Education.

Hattie, John, and Helen Timperley. 2007. "The Power of Feedback." *Review of Educational Research* 77 (1): 81–112.

Heritage, Margaret. 2007. "Formative Assessment: What Do Teachers Need to Know and Do?" *Phi Delta Kappan* 89 (2): 140–46.

Heritage, Margaret. 2013. *Formative Assessment Practice: A Process of Inquiry and Action*. Cambridge, MA: Harvard Education Press.

Herman, Joan L., Ellen Osmundson, and David Silver. 2010. *Capturing Quality in Formative Assessment Practice: Measurement Challenges*. CRESST Report 770. Los Angeles: University of California, Los Angeles, National Center for Research on Evaluation, Standards, and Student Testing (CRESST).

Hiebert, James, Anne K. Morris, Dawn Berk, and Amanda Jansen. 2007. "Preparing Teachers to Learn from Teaching." *Journal of Teacher Education* 58 (1): 47–61.

Honig, Meredith I. 2003. "Building Policy from Practice: District Central Office Administrators' Roles and Capacity for Implementing Collaborative Education Policy." *Educational Administration Quarterly* 39 (3): 292–338.

Horn, Ilana S., and Judith Warren Little. 2009. "Attending to Problems of Practice: Routines and Resources for Professional Learning in Teachers' Workplace Interactions." *American Educational Research Journal* 47 (1): 181–217.

Huinker, DeAnn, and Janis Freckmann. 2009. "Linking Principles of Formative Assessment to Classroom Practice." *Wisconsin Teacher of Mathematics* 60 (2): 6–11.

Jackson, Cara, Amelia Wenk Gotwals, and Beth Tarasawa. 2017. "How to Implement Assessment Literacy." *Principal Leadership* (May). https://www.nassp.org/category/pl/page/52/.

Jeynes, William H. 2005. "A Meta-Analysis of the Relation of Parental Involvement to Urban Elementary School Student Academic Achievement." *Urban Education* 40 (3): 237–69.

Joint Committee on Standards for Educational Evaluation, Don Klinger, Patricia McDivitt, Barbara Howard, Todd Rogers, Marco Muñoz, and Caroline Wylie. 2015. *The Classroom Assessment Standards for PreK-12 Teachers*. Kindle version available at no cost at https://www.amazon.com/Classroom-Assessment-Standards-PreK-12-Teachers-ebook/dp/B00V6C9RVO.

Kagan, Spencer. 1989. "The Structural Approach to Cooperative Learning." *Educational Leadership* 47 (4): 12–15.

Kane, Thomas J., and Douglas O. Staiger. 2012. "Gathering Feedback for Teaching: Combining High-Quality Observations with Student Surveys and Achievement Gains." Research Paper. MET Project. Seattle, WA: Bill & Melinda Gates Foundation. https://files.eric.ed.gov/fulltext/ED540960.pdf.

Kintz, Tara, John Lane, Amelia Wenk Gotwals, and Dante Cisterna. 2015. "Professional Development at the Local Level: Necessary and Sufficient Conditions for Critical Colleagueship." *Teaching and Teacher Education* 51: 121–36.

Klenowski, Val. 2009. "Assessment for Learning Revisited: An Asia-Pacific Perspective." *Assessment in Education: Principles, Policy & Practice* 16: 263–68.

Kraft, Matthew A., and Todd Rogers. 2015. "The Underutilized Potential of Teacher-to-Parent Communication: Evidence from a Field Experiment." *Economics of Education Review* 47: 49–63.

Lampert, Magdelene, and Filippo Graziani. 2009. "Instructional Activities as a Tool for Teachers' and Teacher Educators' Learning." *The Elementary School Journal* 109 (5): 491–509.

Learning Heroes. 2017. "School Report Card Prototype: A Parent Communications Tool." PowerPoint Webinar.

Learning Heroes. 2018. *Parents 2018: Going Beyond Good Grades*. Alexandria, VA: Learning Heroes. https://r50gh2ss1ic2mww8s3uvjvq1-wpengine.netdna-ssl.com/wp-content/uploads/2018/12/2018_Research_Report-final_WEB.pdf.

Levine, Thomas H. 2010. "Tools for the Study and Design of Collaborative Teacher Learning: The Affordances of Different Conceptions of Teacher Community and Activity Theory." *Teacher Education Quarterly* 37 (1): 109–30.

Lewin, Tamar. 2010. "Expansion of A.P. Tests Also Bring More Failures." *The New York Times*, February 10, A19.

Lord, Beth. 1994. "Teachers' Professional Development: Critical Colleagueship and the Role of Professional Communities." In *The Future of Education: Perspectives on National Standards in Education*, edited by Nina Cobb, 175–204. New York, NY: College Entrance Examination Board.

Marion, Scott F. 2018. "The Opportunities and Challenges of a Systems Approach to Assessment." *Educational Measurement: Issues and Practice* 37 (1): 45–48. https://onlinelibrary.wiley.com/doi/abs/10.1111/emip.12193.

Marsh, Julie A. 2012. "Interventions Promoting Educators' Use of Data: Research Insights and Gaps." *Teachers College Record* 114 (11): 1–48.

Marsh, Julie A., Jennifer Sloan McCombs, and Francisco Martorell. 2010. "How Instructional Coaches Support Data-Driven Decision Making: Policy Implications and Effects in Florida Middle Schools." *Educational Policy* 24 (6): 872–907.

Martinez, Felipe, Sandy Taut, and Kevin Schaaf. 2016. "Classroom Observation for Evaluating and Improving Teaching: An International Perspective." *Studies in Educational Evaluation* 49: 15–29.

Marzano, Robert J. 2001. *Designing a New Taxonomy of Educational Objectives*. Thousand Oaks, CA: Corwin.

Marzano, Robert J. 2010. *An Observational Protocol Based on "the Art and Science of Teaching."* Englewood, CO: Marzano Research Laboratory.

Marzano, Robert J., Debra J. Pickering, and Jane E. Pollock. 2001. *Classroom Instruction That Works: Research-Based Strategies for Increasing Student Achievement*. Alexandria, VA: Association for Supervision and Curriculum Development.

Millard Public Schools. "Assessment, Research and Evaluation." Accessed November 30, 2019a. https://sites.google.com/a/mpsomaha.org/mps/departments/dare.

Millard Public Schools. "Leadership and Learning, Professional Learning Communities." Accessed November 30, 2019b. https://leadershipandlearning.mpsomaha.org.

Millard Public Schools. "Superintendent Message." Accessed November 2, 2018. https://www.mpsomaha.org/about/superintendent.

Mintz, Ethan, Sarah A. Fiarman, and Tom Buffett. 2006. "Digging into Data." In *Data Wise: A Step-by-Step Guide to Using Assessment Results to Improve Teaching and Learning*, edited by Kathryn Parker Boudett, Elizabeth A. City, and Richard J. Murnane, 81–96. Cambridge, MA: Harvard Education Press.

Mishkind, Anne. 2014. *Evidence-Based Professional Learning*. Research Brief no. 11. Sacramento: California Department of Education. https://www.calpro-online.org/pubs/evidencebasedprofessionallearning.pdf.

Moss, Pamela A. 2003. "Reconceptualizing Validity for Classroom Assessment." *Educational Measurement: Issues and Practice* 22 (4): 14–16.

Moss, Pamela A. 2008. "Sociocultural Implications for Assessment I: Classroom Assessment." In *Assessment, Equity, and Opportunity to Learn*, edited by Pamela A. Moss, Diana C. Pullin, James Paul Gee, Edward H. Haertel, and Lauren Jones Young, 222–58. Cambridge: Cambridge University Press.

National Assessment Governing Board, Ad Hoc Committee on NAEP Parent Engagement. 2012. *Reaching Parents with NAEP Resources*. Washington, DC: National Assessment Governing Board.

National PTA. n.d. "National Standards for Family-School Partnerships." https://www.pta.org/home/run-your-pta/National-Standards-for-Family-School-Partnerships.

National Task Force on Assessment Education, Northwest Evaluation Association. 2016.

Nebraska Department of Education. 2019. "NSCAS Overview." https://www.education.ne.gov/assessment/nscas-system.

Nebraska State Board of Education. 2018. *Commitments for Equity in Education.* https://cdn.education.ne.gov/wp-content/uploads/2018/07/2018EquityCommitments.pdf.

Nelson, Tamara H., David Slavit, Mart Perkins, and Tom Hathorn. 2008. "A Culture of Collaborative Inquiry: Learning to Develop and Support Professional Learning Communities." *Teachers College Record* 110 (6): 1269–303.

Nelson, Tamara Holmlund, and David Slavit. 2007. "Collaborative Inquiry among Science and Mathematics Teachers in the USA: Professional Learning Experiences through Cross-Grade, Cross-Discipline Dialogue." *Journal of In-Service Education* 33 (1): 23–39.

Newmann, Fred M., M. Bruce King, and Peter Youngs. 2000. "Professional Development that Addresses School Capacity: Lessons from Urban Elementary Schools." *American Journal of Education* 108 (4): 259–99.

Nolen, Susan Bobbitt. 2011. "The Role of Educational Systems in the Link between Formative Assessment and Motivation." *Theory into Practice* 50 (4): 319.

Nolen, Susan Bobbitt, Ilana Seidel Horn, Christopher J. Ward, and Sarah Childers. 2011. "Assessment Tools as Boundary Objects in Novice Teachers' Learning." *Cognition and Instruction* 29 (1): 88–122.

Nungester, Ronald J., and Philippe C. Duchastel. 1982. "Testing versus Review: Effects on Retention." *Journal of Educational Psychology* 74 (1): 18–22.

Ohio Department of Education. 2019. *Ohio's State Tests Interpretive Guide: Grade 3 English Language Arts Family Reports.* https://oh.portal.airast.org/core/fileparse.php/3094/urlt/OST_Spring19_G3_ELA_Guide.pdf.

Oregon Department of Education. 2019. *The Right Assessment for the Right Purpose: Guidance Document.* Salem, OR: Oregon Department of Education. https://www.oregon.gov/ode/educator-resources/assessment/Documents/RightAssessmentRightPurpose.pdf.

Paivio, Allan. 1969. "Mental Imagery in Associative Learning and Memory." *Psychological Review* 76: 241–63.

Pashler, Harold, Mark McDaniel, Doug Rohrer, and Robert Bjork. 2009. "Learning Styles: Concepts and Evidence." *Psychological Science in the Public Interest* 9 (3): 105–19.

Pellegrino, James W., Naomi Chudowsky, and Robert Glaser. 2001. *Knowing What Students Know: The Science and Design of Educational Assessment.* Washington, DC: National Academy Press.

Penuel, William R., and Lorrie A. Shepard. 2016. "Assessment and Teaching." In *Handbook of Research on Teaching*, edited by Drew Gitomer and Courtney Bell. Washington, DC: American Educational Research Association.

Penuel, William R., Barry J. Fishman, Ryoko Yamaguchi, and Lawrence P. Gallagher. 2007. "What Makes Professional Development Effective? Strategies That Foster Curriculum Implementation." *American Educational Research Journal* 44 (4): 921–58.

Pink, Daniel H. 2006. *A Whole New Mind: Why Right-Brainers Will Rule the Future*. New York: Riverhead Books.

Popham, W. James. 2009. "Assessment Literacy for Teachers: Faddish or Fundamental?" *Theory into Practice* 48 (1): 4–11.

Popham, William J. 2008. *Transformative Assessment*. Alexandria, VA: Association for Supervision and Curriculum Development.

Randel, Bruce, and Tedra Clark. 2013. "Measuring Classroom Assessment Practices." In *SAGE Handbook of Research on Classroom Assessment*, edited by James H. McMillan, 145–64. Thousand Oaks, CA: SAGE.

Rhode Island Department of Education and Amplify Education, Inc. 2013. *Data Conversations: Data Use Professional Development Series*. Providence: Rhode Island Department of Education and Amplify Education, Inc. https://www.ride.ri.gov/Portals/0/Uploads/Documents/Instruction-and-Assessment-World-Class-Standards/Instructional-Resources/Data-Use-PD/Turnkey_Data_Conversations.pdf.

Richmond, Emily. 2016. "When Students Lead Parent-Teacher Conferences." *The Hechinger Report*, April 6. https://hechingerreport.org/when-students-lead-parent-teacher-conferences/.

Riley, Michael. 2005. "AP as the 'Common Curriculum.'" College Board AP Central. http://apcentral.collegeboard.com/apc/public/features/18762.html.

Rosenshine, Barak. 2010. *Principles of Instruction*. Geneva, Switzerland: The International Academy of Education.

Roth, Kathleen J., Helen E. Garnier, Catherine Chen, Meike Lemmens, Kathleen Schwille, and Nicole I. Z. Wickler. 2011. "Video Based Lesson Analysis: Effective Science PD for Teacher and Student Learning." *Journal of Research in Science Teaching* 48: 117–48.

Sato, Mistilina. 2003. "Working with Teachers in Assessment-Related Professional Development." In *Everyday Assessment in the Science Classroom*, edited by J. Myron Atkin and Janet E. Coffey, 109–20. Arlington, VA: NSTA Press.

Schildkamp, Kim. 2019. "Data-Based Decision-Making for School Improvement: Research Insights and Gaps." *Educational Research* 61 (3): 257–73. https://doi.org/10.1080/00131881.2019.1625716.

Schneider, Jack. 2009. "Privilege, Equity, and the Advanced Placement Program: Tug of War." *Journal of Curriculum Studies* 41 (6): 813–31.

Schneider, M. Christina, and Bruce Randel. 2009. "Research on Characteristics of Effective Professional Development Programs for Enhancing Educators' Skills in Formative Assessment." In *Handbook of Formative Assessment*, edited by Heidi L. Andrade and Gregory Cizek, 251–76. New York: Routledge.

Shepard, Lorrie A. 2000. "The Role of Assessment in a Learning Culture." *Educational Researcher* 29 (7): 4–14.

Sherrington, Tom. 2019. *Rosenshine's Principles in Action*. Suffolk, England: John Catt Educational Limited.

Smith, John P., Andrea A. diSessa, and Jeremy Roschelle. 1994. "Misconceptions Reconceived: A Constructivist Analysis of Knowledge in Transition." *Journal of the Learning Sciences* 3 (2): 115–63.

Spillane, James P., and David B. Miele. 2007. "Evidence in Practice: A Framing of the Terrain." In *Evidence and Decision Making: 106th Yearbook of the National Society for the Study of Education*, edited by Pamela A. Moss, 46–73. Malden, MA: Blackwell.

Star, Susan Leigh, and James R. Griesemer. 1989. "Institutional Ecology, 'Translations' and Boundary Objects: Amateurs and Professionals in Berkeley's Museum of Vertebrate Zoology, 1907–39." *Social Studies of Science* 19 (3): 392–93.

Steele, Jennifer L., and Jane E. King. 2006. "Planning to Assess Progress." In *Data Wise: A Step-by-Step Guide to Using Assessment Results to Improve Teaching and Learning*, edited by Kathryn Parker Boudett, Elizabeth A. City, and Richard J. Murnane, 137–54. Cambridge, MA: Harvard Education Press.

Stiggins, Rick. 2017. *The Perfect Assessment System*. Alexandria, VA: ASCD.

Stoll, Louise, Ray Bolam, Agnes McMahon, Mike Wallace, and Sally Thomas. 2006. "Professional Learning Communities: A Review of the Literature." *Journal of Educational Change* 7 (4): 221–58.

Stroupe, David, and Amelia Wenk Gotwals. 2018. "'It's 1000 Degrees in Here When I Teach': Providing Preservice Teachers with an Extended Opportunity to Approximate Ambitious Instruction." *Journal of Teacher Education* 69 (3): 294–306.

Sun, Jingping, Robert Przybylski, and Bob J. Johnson. 2016. "A Review of Research on Teachers' Use of Student Data: From the Perspective of School Leadership." *Educational Assessment, Evaluation and Accountability* 28 (1): 5–33.

Sutfin, Jim. "A Message from Dr. Jim Sutfin." Accessed November 30, 2019. https://sites.google.com/a/mpsomaha.org/mps/superintendent.

Tarasawa, Beth, Amelia Wenk Gotwals, and Cara Jackson. 2018. "Seven Successful Strategies for Literate Assessment." *Principal Leadership* (October). National

Association of Secondary School Principals. https://www.nassp.org/2018/10/01/viewpoint-october-2018.

Through the Looking Glass. 2013. *Parents with Disabilities and Their Children: Promoting Inclusion and Awareness in the Classroom*. Berkeley, CA: Through the Looking Glass. https://www.lookingglass.org/pdf/Classroom-Awareness-Parents-with-Disabilities-2013-TLG-.pdf.

Timperley, Helen. 2009. "Evidence-Informed Conversations Making a Difference to Student Achievement." In *Professional Learning Conversations: Challenges in Using Evidence for Improvement*, edited by Lorna M. Earl and Helen Timperley, 69–79. Dordrecht, Netherlands: Springer.

Tsai, Tiffany, and Katie Tosh. 2019. *Educator Access to and Use of Data Systems*. Santa Monica, CA: RAND.

US Department of Education, Office of Planning, Evaluation and Policy Development. 2010. *Use of Education Data at the Local Level: From Accountability to Instructional Improvement*. Washington, DC: US Department of Education.

van Es, Elizabeth A., and Miriam Gamoran Sherin. 2002. "Learning to Notice: Scaffolding New Teachers' Interpretations of Classroom Interactions." *Journal of Technology and Teacher Education* 10 (4): 571–96.

Wayne, Andrew J., Kwang Suk Yoon, Pei Zhu, Stephanie Cronen, and Michael S. Garet. 2008. "Experimenting with Teacher Professional Development: Motives and Methods." *Educational Researcher* 37 (8): 469–79.

Webb, Mary, and Jane Jones. 2009. "Exploring Tensions in Developing Assessment for Learning." *Assessment in Education: Principles, Policy & Practice* 16 (2): 165–84.

Webster-Wright, Ann. 2009. "Reframing Professional Development through Understanding Authentic Professional Learning." *Review of Educational Research* 79 (2): 702–39.

Wei, Ruth Chung, Linda Darling-Hammond, and Frank Adamson. 2010. *Professional Development in the United States: Trends and Challenges*. Dallas, TX: National Staff Development Council.

Wenger, Etienne. 1998. *Communities of Practice: Learning, Meaning, and Identity*. Cambridge, UK: Cambridge University Press.

Wiggins, Grant, and Jay McTighe. 2005. *Understanding by Design*. Alexandria, VA: Association for Supervision and Curriculum Development.

Wiliam, Dylan, and Siobhán Leahy. 2015. *Embedding Formative Assessment: Practical Techniques for K-12 Classrooms*. West Palm Beach, FL: Learning Sciences International.

Wiliam, Dylan, Clare Lee, Christine Harrison, and Paul Black. 2004. "Teachers Developing Assessment for Learning: Impact on Student Achievement." *Assessment in Education: Principles Policy and Practice* 11 (1): 49–65.

Wilson, Suzanne M., and Jennifer Berne. 1999. "Teacher Learning and the Acquisition of Professional Knowledge: An Examination of Research on Contemporary Professional Development." *Review of Research in Education* 24: 173–209.

Windschitl, Mark, Jessica Thompson, Melissa Braaten, and David Stroupe. 2012. "Proposing a Core Set of Instructional Practices and Tools for Teachers of Science." *Science Education* 96 (5): 878–903.

Index

accountability, significance of, vii, xv, 26–28, 49, 86, 106; communication with students and families and, 116, 120, 131, 134; everyday data and, 6, 14, 20
Accountability for a Quality Education System Today and Tomorrow (AQuESTT), 27
Adaptive Schools Foundation Training, 100, 102
Advanced Placement (AP) courses, 37–38, 84
agency, of student, 130–33
AIR. *See* American Institutes for Research (AIR)
Air Force Junior ROTC, 28
Alpine Achievement system, 132
ambitious teaching, 2
American Educator Panels survey, 25
American Institutes for Research (AIR), 123
American Welding Society (AWS) certification tests, 13
AP. *See* Advanced Placement (AP) courses
AQuESTT. *See* Accountability for a Quality Education System Today and Tomorrow (AQuESTT)

assessment and teaching, integration of, 43; assessment as guide to teaching and, 46–47 (course teaching determination, 48–50; goal setting and remediation approach determination, 51–53; grouping decisions to address educational needs, 51; pacing lessons, 50–51; student educational needs and support, 53–54; student strength and weakness identification, 48; success celebration, 54–55); assessment as teaching and, 55–56 (cognitive psychology in classroom, 56; distributed practice, 57–59; dual coding, 59–60; implications, 60–61; testing effect, 56–57); research base for, 43 (assessment to plan teaching, 43–44; assessment to support responsive teaching, 44–45; fostering student engagement in learning process, 45–46; successful teaching determination, 45)
assessment designing, aligning with clear learning targets, 67–68
assessment development cycle, 69
assessment literacy, xix–xxi; case study for, 9–10 (biomedical science,

10–11; welding, 12–13); continuum, 13–14; course, and clear learning targets, 65–73 (alignment within and across standards, 73–74; assessment matching and balancing, 79–80; packaging targets and assessment at unit level, 80–81; scope and sequence and learning activities, 74, 77; teacher response to classifying learning targets, 77–79); definition of, xix; across Maryland, 106–7 (Educator Effectiveness Academies/Maryland College and Career Ready Conferences project, 107–10; FAME influence, 111–14; Maryland Assessment Literacy Collaborative (MALC), 110–11); in Millard Public Schools, 29–31

Assessment Literacy Specialization course, 72

assessment planning and design, 68–70

assessment practice: dual coding theory and, 60; teacher negotiation with, 33 (administrators, 35–36; colleagues, 35; external audiences, 36–37; grading practices, 37–40; multiple context layers, 40; novice teachers, 34; students, 34–35)

assignment field experience, 69–70

AWS. *See* American Welding Society (AWS) certification tests

Baltimore County Public Schools, 111
Beck, Cherissa, 112
benchmark assessment, 27, 45
Berger, Ron, 116
Berne, Jennifer, 96
bias, 31; attention to, 88
Black, Paul, 2, 3
Bloom, Benjamin S., 91
boundary objects, assessment objects as, 33

CAEP. *See* Council for the Accreditation of Educator Programs (CAEP)

California Department of Education, 111

card assessment, for students, 46–51; daily, 48; and end-of-the-week quizzes compared, 50; exit, 49; formal and informal, significance of, 50; grouping decisions and, 51; hallmarks of, 54; reading, 49, 51

Career Academies, 28

CCSSO. *See* Council of Chief State Schools Officers (CCSSO)

The Center for Advanced Technical Studies, 5–8; assessment literacy at, 9–13 (continuum, 13–14); quality data access at, 8–9; relational trust at, 8; shared vision at, 7; study programs of, 6, 7

Chappuis, Jan, 77

Classroom Assessment Scoring System (CLASS), 45

classroom walkthrough observations, importance of, 90–92

CMAS. *See* Colorado Measures of Academic Success (CMAS)

Coburn, Cynthia E., 23, 24

Cognitive Coaching Foundation Seminar, 100, 102

collaboration, 82, 91, 93, 139, 141; assessment and teaching integration and, 49, 51, 61; communication with students and families and, 119–20, 129; context and, 23–25, 29, 32; everyday data and, 1, 6, 9–10, 16, 17, 19; with colleagues, 95–98, 103, 107–11

colleagues, working with, 95; assessment literacy across Maryland and, 106–7; (Educator Effectiveness Academies/Maryland College and Career Ready Conferences project, 107–11; FAME influence, 111–14; Maryland Assessment Literacy Collaborative (MALC), 110–11); FAME case study and, 98–106; professional learning communities (PLCs) and, 96–97 (collaborative

Index

learning about assessment and, 97–98)
Colorado Department of Education, 135
Colorado Measures of Academic Success (CMAS), 12
Commission to Review Maryland's Use of Assessments in Public Schools, 110
community outreach: community educational specialists and, 133–34; instructional coaches and, 134; Parent Academy for Student Success (PASS) program, 134
Competency Tracker, 133
context creation, for everyday data use support, 4–5
continuous improvement process, 15–16, 20; assessment practice and, 14; formative assessment for, 73; mutual respect and, 25
Core Knowledge Program, 28
Council for the Accreditation of Educator Programs (CAEP), 74
Council of Chief State School Officers (CCSSO), 45, 85, 110, 138
Creating Clear Learning Targets course, 72, 73

Danielson Group Framework for Teaching, 45, 63
data coach, importance of, 15
data notebook, 133
Data Quality Campaign, 124–25
data triangulation, 20
data use framework, 23–24
data-use routines, 24
Data Wise process (Harvard University), 15–16
Datnow, Amanda, 45
decision making structure, 38–39
DESE. *See* Massachusetts Department of Elementary and Secondary Education (DESE)
dialogue, as data, 2–3
differentiated professional development resources, 13–14

Diploma Programme (DP) International Baccalaureate program, 28
diSessa, Andrea A., 2
distributed practice, 57–59
district and school context, understanding of, 89
DiVasto, Patricia, 19
dual coding, 59–60
Duchastel, Philippe C., 57
du Pont, Henry B., 121

Early College High School, 28
Ebbinghaus, Hermann, 58
Edge Research, Tembo, and HCM Strategists, 120
Educator Effectiveness Academies/ Maryland College and Career Ready Conferences project, 107–11
educators, empowering, 90–92
Empower digital reporting and recording system, 131–32, 135
equitable teaching and learning, everyday data as tool for. *See* Rancho Public Schools (RRPS)
everyday data, in new ways: case study (The Center for Advanced Technical Studies, 5–14; Rio Rancho Public Schools (RRPS), 14–21); research base for, 1–5
exit slips, 46, 47, 86, 139

FAME. *See* Formative Assessment for Michigan Educators (FAME)
feedback, xvii, 7, 11, 93, 103, 108, 138; assessment and teaching integration and, 44–53, 57; communication with students and families and, 116, 120, 123, 127, 128, 134; immediate and specific, 12–13; learning targets clarification and, 64, 70–71, 81–82; timely, 27
formative assessment, xvi–xviii, 3, 54, 83, 138; The Center for Advanced Technical Studies, 8, 9, 14; for continuous improvement, 73; definition of, 85; distributed practice

and, 58; Maryland Assessment Literacy Collaborative (MALC) and, 110–11; for Maryland Educators project, 108–10; Millard Public Schools and, 28; practices of, 10; professional learning communities (PLCS) and, 97–98; Rio Rancho Public Schools (RRPS), 17, 19; unit test blueprint for, 80. *See also* Formative Assessment for Michigan Educators (FAME); purpose-driven assessments
"Formative Assessment for Leadership Teams", 113
Formative Assessment for Michigan Educators (FAME), 98–99; administrative support in Hesperia and, 101–2; coach background and, 100–101; district approach for, 102–3; future plans of, 105–6; influence on assessment literacy, 111–13; Learning Teams, 100, 103–5; professional learning model, 100; progress status of, 104–5; to support ongoing teacher learning, 100; working of, 103–4
Freckmann, Janis, 64
From Puzzle to Plan (Learning Heroes), 128

Gallup, 117
Garcia, Maria E., 127–28
Gates, Al, 7–8
Gibbs, Elise, 18, 19
goal-setting sheets, 133
grade-level goals, 28, 30–37, 46–48, 93, 101; communication with students and families and, 123–30, 134–35; everyday data and, 9, 14–19; practices, 37–40
Grant High School (Portland, Oregon), 128–29

Hain, Bonnie, 112
Harvard Family Research Project, 118

Hesperia Community Schools (Hesperia, Michigan), 100–102, 105
Hiebert, James, 44
high-stakes assessment results, communication of, 134–35
Huinker, DeAnn, 64

IEPs. *See* Individualized Education Plans (IEPs)
implicit learning, significance of, 13–14
Individualized Education Plans (IEPs), 121
innovation, 5, 7, 29, 31, 65
instructional coaches, 4, 134
InTASC. *See* Interstate Teacher Assessment and Support Consortium (InTASC)
interim assessment, 8–10, 14, 15, 17–21, 27, 28, 117; significance of, 17
Interstate Teacher Assessment and Support Consortium (InTASC): Model Core Teaching Standards, 45; Standards, 74

Jeynes, William H., 116
Junior Academy for the Advancement of Science, 11
Junior Science and Humanities Symposium, 11

Kagan, Spencer, 101
Kane, Thomas J., 45
Kennedy-Lewis, Brianna, 45
King, Jane E., 3

"Launching into Learning" sessions, 100
Leahy, Siobhán, 3
learning continuum, significance of, 18–19
Learning Forward Foundation, 112
Learning Heroes, 120, 128
learning styles theory, 59
learning targets, 63, 131; clarity in, 65–66 (assessment matching and

Index

balancing, 79–80; course outline, 66–72; learning targets alignment within and across standards, 73–74; packaging targets and assessment at unit level, 80–81; scope and sequence and learning activities, 74, 77; teacher response to classifying learning targets, 77–79); course, alignment matrix for, 75–76; definition of, 63; effective, 64–65; student efficacy modeling through candidate efficacy and, 81–82

MABE. *See* Maryland Association of Boards of Education (MABE)
MAC. *See* Michigan Assessment Consortium (MAC)
MAG. *See* Maryland Assessment Group (MAG)
MALC. *See* Maryland Assessment Literacy Collaborative (MALC)
Marion, Scott F., 27
Marsh, Julie A., 17, 25, 26
Maryland Assessment Group (MAG), 112
Maryland Assessment Literacy Collaborative (MALC), 110
Maryland Association of Boards of Education (MABE), 110
Maryland State Department of Education (MSDE), 108, 109, 110
Marzano, Robert, 64, 91, 101
Massachusetts Department of Elementary and Secondary Education (DESE), 126
MDE. *See* Michigan Department of Education (MDE)
memory consolidation, 56–58
Michigan Assessment Consortium (MAC), 98
Michigan Department of Education (MDE), 98, 99, 100, 103
Middle Years Programme (MYP), 28
Miller, Christina, 113

motivation, xix, 45, 90, 101, 128, 141; context and, 23, 38–40
MSDE. *See* Maryland State Department of Education (MSDE)
Multi-Tiered Systems of Support (MTSS), 27
MYP. *See* Middle Years Programme (MYP)
myths, about assessment, xvi–xix, 137–42

National Assessment Governing Board, 117
National Science Fair, 11
National Standards for Family-School Partnerships, 119
National Task Force on Assessment Education, xix, 87
National University (San Diego), 138
Nebraska Department of Education (NDE), 27, 28
Nebraska Quality Education Systems for Today and Tomorrow (NEQuESTT), 27, 30
Nebraska State Board of Education, 27
Nebraska Student Centered Assessment System (NSCAS), 27
NEQuESTT. *See* Nebraska Quality Education Systems for Today and Tomorrow (NEQuESTT)
Northwest Evaluation Association (NWEA), xix, 117
noticing, aspects of, 2
NSCAS. *See* Nebraska Student-Centered Assessment System (NSCAS)
Nungester, Ronald J., 57
NWEA. *See* Northwest Evaluation Association (NWEA)

The Observational Protocol Based on the Art and Science of Teaching, 63–64
ODE. *See* Ohio Department of Education (ODE)

OFAST. *See* Oregon Formative Assessment for Students and Teachers (OFAST)
Ohio Department of Education (ODE), 122, 126
one-to-one conversations, significance of, 52
Oregon Department of Education, xv–xvi
Oregon Formative Assessment for Students and Teachers (OFAST), 111
organizational and political contexts, 23–26; Millard Public Schools, 26–33; teacher negotiation on assessment practice and, 33–40

PARCC. *See* Partnership for Assessment of Readiness for College and Careers (PARCC)
Parent Academy for Student Success (PASS) program, 134
parents and families, engagement with. *See* students and families, communication with
parent-teacher conferences. *See* students and families, communication with
Park, Vicki, 45
Partnership for Assessment of Readiness for College and Careers (PARCC), 109
PASS. *See* Parent Academy for Student Success (PASS) program
peer teaching, 12–13
Penuel, William R., 43
Pickering, Debra J., 64
Piranha Pond model, 11
PLATO. *See* Protocol for Language Arts Teaching Observations (PLATO) Prime
PLC. *See* professional learning community (PLC)
Pollock, Jane E., 64
Primary Years Programme (PYP), 28
problem-based learning, 6, 10
professional development sessions, importance of, 91–93

professional learning community (PLC), 29–30; components (appropriateness, 31; bias, 31; essential learner outcomes, 30; opportunity to learn, 30; reliability, 31–32; standard setting process, 32; validity, 31); effective, characteristics of, 96–98
project-based learning, 6, 10
Protocol for Language Arts Teaching Observations (PLATO) Prime, 45
PSAT, 132
purpose-driven assessments, 83–85, 87; collective support and, 92–94; educator empowerment for, 90–92; equity promotion for, 88; positive culture fostering for, 88–90; student learning evidence for decision maker and, 85–86
PYP. *See* Primary Years Programme (PYP)

quality data, access to, 8–9
quizzes, 34, 46–55, 139, 140

Race to the Top (RTTT) projects, 107
RAND Corporation, 25
research process, explaining and refining, 10–11
responsive teaching, assessment to support, 44–45
retrieval practice. *See* testing effect
Rhode Island Department of Education (RIDE), 127
Rio Rancho (New Mexico), 139
Rio Rancho Public Schools (RRPS), 14–15; district process, 15–17; lessons learned, 20–21; Sandia Vista Elementary School and, 17–20
Roschelle, Jeremy, 2
Rosenshine, Barak, 2
RRPS. *See* Rio Rancho Public Schools (RRPS)
RTTT. *See* Race to the Top (RTTT) projects
rubric, 45, 64, 65, 86, 140; context and, 29, 31, 32, 35, 36

Sandia Vista Elementary School, 17–20, 140
San Diego County Office of Education, 111
Sauers, Heather, 113
Scantron Performance Series, 132
SCASS. *See* State Collaborative on Assessment and Student Standards (SCASS)
Schildkamp, Kim, 4
School District Five of Lexington and Richland Counties (District 5), 5, 9, 13, 139
school-family partnership strengthening and National PTA recommendations, 119–20, 141; high-quality and family-friendly information and, 121–27; ongoing engagement, 127–30; transparency and trust and, 120–21
School Improvement Team (SIT), 92
school leader, importance of, 4
school norms, 25
Selekman, Aaron, 120–21
self-assessment, to build learning ownership, 4
shared norms and values, significance of, 96
Shepard, Lorrie A., 43
Sherin, Miriam Gamoran, 2
Sherrington, Tom, 2, 45
SIT. *See* School Improvement Team (SIT)
Smith, John P., 2
social-emotional impacts, of testing, 71–72
South Carolina Graduate Profile, 5–6, 18
South Carolina Junior Academy of Science, 11
spaced practice. *See* distribution practice
SRG. *See* Standards-Referenced Grading (SRG)
staff buy-in, importance of, 104
Staiger, Douglas O., 45

Standards-Referenced Grading (SRG), 40
State Collaborative on Assessment and Student Standards (SCASS), 110; Formative Assessment for Students and Teachers (FAST), 110
Steele, Jennifer L., 3
Stiggins, Rick, 23, 70, 71, 72
strategic questioning, 86, 139–40
student agency, 130–33
Student Data Picture, 133
student engagement fostering, in learning process, 45–46
student learning outcomes (SLOs). *See* learning targets
student-led conferences, significance of, 116–17, 141
students and families, communication with, 115–19; school-family partnership strengthening and National PTA recommendations, 119–20 (high-quality and family-friendly information, 121–27; ongoing engagement with parents and families, 127–30; transparency and trust, 120–21); Westminster Public Schools and student empowerment and, 130–36
students' thinking in learning process, eliciting role of, 2–3
student strengths and weaknesses, identifying, 48
student work, 3–4
summative assessment, xvi, xviii, 3, 8, 9, 16, 83, 105; distributed practice and, 58; high-stakes, 134–35; practices of, 10, 90; unit test blueprint for, 80
Superstar Assessment infomercials, 91

Teacher Leaders, 29–32
testing effect, 56–58, 139; and cognitive psychology, 57; distribution of, 58
tests and assessment, xvii. *See also individual entries*
think-aloud protocols, 39

thumbs up/thumbs down, 86, 139
Toolkit of Resources for Engaging Families and the Community as Partners in Education: Part 4, 127–28
trust, culture of, 8
Turner, Erica O., 23, 24

US Department of Education, 25

van Es, Elizabeth A., 2

Westminster Public Schools (WPS), 130, 141; Alpine Achievement system and, 132; challenges for, 135–36; community outreach, 133–34; Competency-Based System (CBS), 130–31, 136 (Performance Level Placement, 132); high-stakes assessment results communication and, 134–35; purposeful strategies empowering students and families and, 135; reporting, recording, and trainings and, 131–32; student agency, 132–33
West Virginia Department of Education (WVDE), 123–25
WIDA ACCESS, 132
Wiliam, Dylan, 2, 3
Wilson, Suzanne M., 96
WPS. *See* Westminster Public Schools (WPS)
WVDE. *See* West Virginia Department of Education (WVDE)

Young, Kim, 99

About the Editors

Dr. Beth Tarasawa is the executive vice president of research at NWEA where she leads a talented team of researchers who are devoted to transforming education research through advancements in assessment, growth measurement, and the availability of longitudinal data. Her research focuses on issues related to educational equity, particularly those concerning social class, race, and linguistic diversity.

Her work has been funded by the National Science Foundation, the American Sociological Association, and The Spencer Foundation, and featured by *PBS NewsHour*, Children's Institute, *The Hechinger Report*, *The Atlantic*, and New America. Dr. Tarasawa also teaches in the Department of Educational Leadership & Policy in the Graduate School of Education at Portland State University. Prior to NWEA, she was a faculty member at Washington State University and St. Norbert College. She completed a PhD in sociology of education from Emory University with a concentration in education policy.

About the Editors

Dr. Cara Jackson is an associate partner with Bellwether Education Partners, focusing on issues related to evaluation and planning, research design, survey research, and quantitative data analysis. She provides technical assistance and supports capacity building related to program evaluation and quasi-experimental analysis. Dr. Jackson is also an adjunct lecturer at American University's School of Education, where she teaches research methods.

Previously, Dr. Jackson worked as an evaluation specialist for Montgomery County Public Schools, where she designed and conducted studies to inform district policies. She also has experience developing and refining teacher evaluation systems as the assistant director of research and evaluation for Urban Teachers and conducting studies of federal education policy as a senior analyst at the US Government Accountability Office. Earlier in her career, Dr. Jackson taught prekindergarten and kindergarten in New York City. She earned her PhD in education policy and an advanced certificate in education measurement, statistics, and evaluation from the University of Maryland. Her master's degree is from the Harvard Graduate School of Education, where she is also an alum of the Strategic Data Project Fellowship. Dr. Jackson currently serves on the board of the Association for Education Finance and Policy.

Dr. Amelia Wenk Gotwals is an associate professor of teacher education at Michigan State University. In this role, she teaches undergraduate science methods classes for preservice teachers and quantitative methods classes for graduate students. Her research focuses on supporting teachers in developing ambitious instructional practices especially around formative assessment and science literacy. She is particularly interested in developing research practice partnerships with teachers and districts as they work on implementing the

Next Generation Science Standards. Her work has been funded by the National Science Foundation, The Spencer Foundation, and the Michigan Department of Education (MDE).

Dr. Gotwals began her career as a middle school and high school science teacher in Maryland and New Jersey. She earned a master's degree in Ecology and Evolutionary Biology and a PhD in educational studies, with a focus in science education, both from the University of Michigan.

About the Contributors

CHAPTER 1

Mary Ellen (Missy) Wall-Mitchell has worked in the education measurement field for over thirty years. She recently retired from the Lexington/Richland School District in South Carolina, where she directed the assessment, research, and evaluation programs. She provides consulting services to schools and districts in assessment literacy, strategic planning, and SAS programming. Prior to working in education measurement, she studied and worked in the areas of biostatistics and marine biology.

Dr. Happy Miller serves as the executive director for research, assessment, data and accountability for Rio Rancho Public Schools (RRPS) in New Mexico. Together with her colleagues, she strives to facilitate the implementation of a balanced assessment system and to help a variety of stakeholders more effectively use the information to improve student outcomes. This includes working to improve the district's assessment and data management tools, data interoperability capabilities, and data governance processes.

Dr. Miller currently participates in the national Data Governance Collaborative and several statewide assessment and data advisory councils. She previously participated in the National Task Force for Assessment Education from 2014 to 2018. A former ESL and reading teacher and principal, Dr. Miller has received several honors including the CCSSO State Teacher of the Year award for the Commonwealth of the Northern Mariana Islands in 2002 and a New Mexico School Board Association Excellence in Student Achievement Award in 2014.

Beata I. Thorstensen has spent the better part of the last two decades working with school principals and teachers on using accountability data for the purposes of school improvement. She has worked on issues of large-scale assessment and accountability at the national, state, and local levels. Her favorite work is that which she engages in now, working to build effective, high-functioning teams that can use data quickly and effectively to guide changes to instruction, leading to more positive outcomes for students for RRPS.

CHAPTER 2

Bernice Stafford is an independent consultant. Her career spans more than four decades in the public and private sectors of the education industry in the United States and abroad. She has been a classroom teacher, early childhood administrator, college lecturer, corporate executive, company cofounder, and strategic consultant. She is an expert in aligning business strategies and goals with educator professional learning including expert and peer coaching in assessment literacy, education policy, funding, and instructional technology.

She is a recognized leader in the education industry, serving or having served on the boards of national and international organizations, including WestEd, Inflexion (formerly EPIC), the Center for Interactive Learning and Collaboration (CILC), the Knowledge Alliance, and Software and Information Industry Association (SIIA). In her home state of California, she also served on the Public Schools Accountability Act (PSAA) Committee.

Ms. Stafford is a frequent presenter on topics ranging from effective implementation of the school transformation process to using state-of-the-art technology and formative assessments in support of teaching and learning. She is also the coauthor of a chapter in the second edition of *International Handbook on Literacy and Technology*.

Dr. Darin Kelberlau's career in education spans twenty-five years, all in Nebraska. The first ten years were as a high school mathematics teacher. The remaining years have been at the district office in a variety of roles, including technology integration, professional learning, assessment leadership, data coaching, curriculum design and leadership, and program evaluation.

Dr. Kelberlau completed the Nebraska Assessment Cohort at the University of Nebraska–Lincoln (UNL), which is an 18-hour graduate program focused on increasing the assessment literacy of teachers and administrators, improving classroom assessment practices, and preparing teachers for leadership roles. After completing the assessment program he became a teaching assistant for six years. In his current role as the executive director of assessment, research, and evaluation for the Millard Public Schools, his major responsibilities include directing the assessment system; collecting, analyzing, interpreting data; and designing program evaluations.

Dr. Kelberlau holds a PhD in quantitative, qualitative, and psychometric methods in education. He earned an MSEd in curriculum and instruction with an emphasis in instructional technology and a BA in mathematics. He also is currently an adjunct professor in the department of Educational Administration at the University of Nebraska–Kearney, where he teaches graduate courses in assessment leadership.

Dr. Susan Bobbitt Nolen is professor emeritus in the College of Education, University of Washington, Seattle. She was the associate director of the UW Secondary Teacher Education Program from 2006 to 2010. A former classroom teacher, her research interests include designing environments to support engagement and how motivation to learn develops over time in social contexts. Most recently she has worked within a sociocultural framework to understand why

people take up or reject social practices, including assessment practices, and how motives arise in social interaction. She coauthored, with Catherine Taylor, the textbook *Classroom Assessment: Supporting Teaching and Learning in Real Classrooms* and has written various articles on assessment practice and policy.

Dr. Susan Cooper received her PhD in Educational Psychology-Learning Sciences and Human Cognition in June 2017. She received her MEd from the University of California, Los Angeles, in 1987, and since then has taught for more than twenty years in public schools and, more recently, at the college level.

At the University of Washington, she taught and coached teacher candidates in the Secondary Teacher Education Program. Dr. Cooper was also a research assistant for the University of Washington's Knowledge in Action Project investigating Project-based Learning in Advanced Placement (AP) Courses in poverty-impacted schools. Her work looks at the decision-making processes of teachers in poverty-impacted schools while they are in the process of summatively assessing their students. Her areas of expertise include formative and summative assessment ethical decision-making processes and how they are inseparable from planning and instruction, motivation and engagement, teacher education, special education, and adolescent development and learning specifically at the middle school level.

Originally from Los Angeles, Dr. Cooper received her BA and MEd from UCLA in 1986 and 1987, respectively. She has been a bilingual classroom teacher, a special education teacher, and a general education social studies and English teacher in public middle schools. She currently is an instructor at Seattle University.

About the Contributors

CHAPTER 3

Scott Reed is a physics teacher at Niles North High School in Skokie, IL. During his tenure, Scott has been recognized as a Golden Apple Teacher of Distinction and Fellow, Chicago Mayor Daley Teacher of Excellence, Argonne National Laboratory QuarkNet Fellow, and Niles North Teacher of the Year. A National Board Certified Teacher in Science, Mr. Reed has led cohorts of prospective teachers from the Golden Apple Summer Institutes on various Chicagoland university campuses for the past decade. Mr. Reed holds master's degrees in curriculum and instruction and teacher leadership from the University of Illinois.

Even after twenty-two years of teaching, Mr. Reed's enthusiasm for inspiring students to augment and advance their abilities as scientists, critical thinkers, and problem solvers remains as strong as ever. Every student in Mr. Reed's classes has an essential voice, and all are needed for the class to achieve their collective high goals and expectations that are driven by the uniqueness of each class and of each student. Compelling questions, inquiry-based activities, lively discussion, ongoing individualized assessment, and thoughtful "real-time" teacher reflection are all hallmarks of Mr. Reed's classes.

Dr. Kim Walters-Parker, PhD, JD, is a former high school teacher, higher education faculty member, and state education agency director. As a high school teacher, Dr. Walters-Parker served primarily as a reading specialist in the Fayette County (Kentucky) Public Schools. Before taking on her state leadership role as the director of educator preparation for the state of Kentucky, Dr. Walters-Parker taught in the education department's literacy specialist program and the political science department's prelaw program at Georgetown College. Dr. Walters-Parker served as an accreditation site visitor, chair of the Accreditation Council of the Council for the Accreditation of Educator Preparation (CAEP), and member of the CAEP Board of Directors. She has presented at state and national conferences on a variety of topics including developing a district-run literacy specialist endorsement program, disciplinary literacy integration, developing and implementing a co-teaching requirement in student teaching, teacher induction, and interoperability of data systems for states and higher education.

CHAPTER 4

Dee L. Fabry, PhD, is professor emeritus, National University, Sanford College of Education in La Jolla, California. She continues to serve as adjunct faculty in the Advanced Assessment Literacy Specialization. She served the university as the associate provost, University Academic Assessment Committee chair, Sanford College of Education coordinator of assessment services, and program lead for the Masters of Science in Advanced Teaching Practices. She was a project manager for test development for Kaplan Learning

in New York and vice president of assessment programs for Plato Learning. She was appointed to the National Assessment in Education Task Force where she contributed regularly to the blogs on effective formative assessment.

Dr. Fabry has over twenty peer-reviewed articles published on effective assessment in teacher education, including "Using Student Online Course Evaluations to Inform Pedagogy." She authored two books: *Opening Doors to Reading* and *On Teaching Well*. She received a Presidential Scholar Award as well as the Presidential Professoriate Award.

Mark LaCelle-Peterson, EdD, is president and CEO of the Association for Advancing Quality in Educator Preparation (AAQEP), a quality assurance agency that provides national accreditation in educator preparation. He has taught and provided leadership in public and private colleges and universities. He served as president of the Teacher Education Accreditation Council (TEAC) and as senior vice president of the American Association of Colleges for Teacher Education (AACTE). With Dr. Fabry, he served on the National Task Force on Assessment Education.

CHAPTER 5

Kathy Dyer is the manager of Learning and Innovation, Professional Learning Design, at NWEA, a research-based, not-for-profit organization specializing in assessment solutions that precisely measure student growth and achievement and that provide insights to help tailor instruction. Kathy served as a public school teacher, principal, district assessment coordinator, and adjunct professor before joining NWEA in 2009. In her current role, she researches, designs, and delivers professional learning opportunities for educators across the United States and around the world.

Ms. Dyer combines a deep understanding of adult learning with a passion for collaborative problem solving to help school systems improve student outcomes. She's committed to furthering the assessment literacy of educators, including strengthening formative assessment practices in classrooms. A frequent conference presenter, Ms. Dyer has had work featured in *eSchool News*, *Education Dive*, *Ed Circuit*, *Getting Smart*, and the NWEA blog, *Teach. Learn. Grow.* She holds an MA in educational leadership from the University of Colorado Denver and a BS in history from Middle Tennessee State University.

Dr. Jennifer M. Hein is the executive director of Strategic Initiatives, Assessment and Accreditation and the director of the South Carolina Teaching Fellows program in the College of Education at Clemson University in Clemson, South Carolina. Dr. Hein has more than nineteen years of experience teaching at the prekindergarten through twelfth grade and university levels. In addition, her experience includes working at a state department of education, serving as an assistant principal and principal, creating and leading programs that support teacher growth and retention, and monitoring student progress and program impact. Jennifer is a staunch advocate of using data to make decisions centered on equity and what is best for students. She provides data literacy support focused on program and learning outcome

improvement. Dr. Hein is highly engaged in organizations such as TransformSC, SC Education Policy Fellows, SC Education Dean's Alliance, and other organizations involved in education advocacy.

CHAPTER 6

Denny Chandler has been part of the Formative Assessment for Michigan Educators (FAME) program since 2008, first as a "coach of coaches" with Measured Progress and later as part of the FAME Research and Development Team. He values the opportunity FAME gives him to contribute to the improvement of education in a positive way. "I've enjoyed all of my experiences with FAME; I especially like contributing to the creation of resources that teachers can actually use to help improve their instruction and help students learn."

Melissa Spadin currently serves as the director of systems of support at the San Diego County Office of Education, providing leadership in Multi-tiered Systems of Support (MTSS), Local Control and Accountability Plan (LCAP), continuous improvement, and implementation science. She first came to the county office as the coordinator of assessment, accountability and evaluation, where she

helped improve assessment literacy across southern California. Prior to this role, she was an assessment program specialist and National Assessment of Educational Progress (NAEP) state coordinator with the Division of Curriculum, Research, Assessment and Accountability at the Maryland State Department of Education (MSDE). As part of the Formative Assessment Team at MSDE, she implemented and sustained the Formative Assessment for Maryland Educators (FAME) professional learning program.

Ms. Spadin was a member of the National Task Force for Assessment Education, which provides thought leadership and resources to improve understanding of assessment and its role in supporting student success. She began her career in education as a high school English and theater teacher, forensics coach, and theater director at Gaithersburg High School in Montgomery County, Maryland.

Heather Lageman serves as the executive director of organizational development for Baltimore County Public Schools. Earlier, she served as the director of curriculum for the MSDE and managed statewide implementation of the Teacher Induction Program. During Race to the Top (RTTT), she served as RTTT Local Education Agency (LEA) director for Maryland and managed both programmatic and fiscal aspects of district projects.

Ms. Lageman is dedicated to supporting the professional learning and development of inspired and innovative educators through her work with nonprofits. She is the Maryland Codes Code.org Regional Partnership program manager, president of the Council of Educational Administrative and Supervisory Organizations of Maryland (CEASOM), and was the facilitator of the Networks and the Internet Writing Team for the K–12 Computer Science Framework. Ms. Lageman serves on the governor's P–20 Leadership Council of Maryland and is a member of the governor's Cybersecurity and Information Technology Task Force. She is

on the board of the Maryland Assessment Group (MAG) and was a member of the National Task Force on Assessment Education. President of Maryland Affiliate of the Association for Supervision and Curriculum Development (ASCD), she is a former president of the Learning Forward Maryland Affiliate and chair of the Learning Forward Foundation.

CHAPTER 7

Jacki Ball is the director of government affairs at National PTA, where she leads PTA's federal policy, advocacy, and lobbying efforts. Prior to joining National PTA, she was the associate director of advocacy at the National Association of Secondary School Principals (NASSP). Ms. Ball has spent her entire career in either the classroom or advocating on behalf of children, families, and educational equity. She started her career as a history and government teacher in Fairfax, Virginia. She has worked on Capitol Hill as a legislative aide and also served as manager of government relations for Reading is Fundamental (RIF). She is an active member of Women in Government Relations (WGR) serving as treasurer for the board of directors and member of the Education Task Force. Ms. Ball has a bachelor's degree from Wake Forest University and a master's degree from the University of Florida.

Chadwick Anderson is employed as the director of culturally and linguistically diverse education for Westminster Public Schools (WPS), a school district with a unique competency-based education system. Previously, he served as principal of Scott Carpenter Middle School, a diverse urban Title

I school in North Denver, for four years. Prior to that he was principal of F.M. Day Elementary in the same school district for five years. Before becoming an administrator, Mr. Anderson worked as a bilingual elementary teacher for fifteen years in Denver and Albuquerque. Mr. Anderson has written various articles and presented at conferences around the country on educational topics such as assessment literacy, culturally responsive instruction, and competency-based education. An avid skier and cyclist, Mr. Anderson resides in the foothills of the Rocky Mountains with a blended family of six kids.

Alison Mund has twenty years of experience in the education field. In this time, she has held a variety of positions, including classroom teacher and instructional coach, and is now moving into administration. Ms. Mund was a part of the change process as WP moved from a traditional educational system to a competency-based system (CBS). This experience provided her with the opportunity to work with many talented professionals to fine-tune classroom instruction and meet the needs of all learners. As a result of this experience, her classroom became a model for other educators to see CBS in action. Additionally, she is involved in planning and facilitating sessions for district symposiums and helping to coach other teachers in the implementation of CBS.

www.ingramcontent.com/pod-product-compliance
Lightning Source LLC
Chambersburg PA
CBHW052100300426
44117CB00013B/2216